ANNA RITCHIE

PICTS

AN INTRODUCTION TO THE LIFE OF THE PICTS
AND THE CARVED STONES IN THE CARE OF THE
SECRETARY OF STATE FOR SCOTLAND

As illustrative materials of unwritten
history, they (Pictish stones) are as
valuable as the seals and the monumental
effigies of later times. They illustrate the
most ancient life in Scotland of which we
have any illustrations.

Joseph Anderson
Scotland in Early Christian Times (1881)

HISTORIC BUILDINGS AND MONUMENTS

EDINBURGH
HER MAJESTY'S STATIONERY OFFICE

2

CONTENTS

Note: Those monuments in state care mentioned in the book are shown in **bold** type. Reference to any other site does not imply public access.

Front Cover
Storytelling in stone: the royal hunt begins (**Meigle**).

Back Cover
Made of jet for a Christian Pict, this pendant was found near Beauly (now in Inverness Art Gallery and Museum).

Inside Front Cover
The museum at **Meigle** (Perth and Kinross) displays some outstanding examples of Pictish sculpture.

Opposite
The cross-slab at **Eassie** (Angus) has recently been cleaned and conserved and is displayed within the ruins of the parish church.

Edited by Christopher Tabraham
Principal photography by David Henrie
Designed by HMSO/GD

HMSO Publications are available from:
HMSO Bookshop
71 Lothian Road, Edinburgh EH3 9AZ
Telephone (031) 228 4181

HMSO Publications Centre
(mail and telephone orders only)
PO Box 276. London SW8 5DT
Telephone orders (01) 873 9090
General enquiries (01) 873 0011

*Other HMSO bookshops and
HMSO's Accredited Agents*
(see Yellow Pages) and through good booksellers

ISBN 0 11 493491 6

MYTH AND REALITY

WHO WERE THE PICTS?

EVER since they were first called *Picti*, 'the Painted Ones', by the Roman soldiers along Hadrian's Wall, the Picts have been the subject of myth and misconception. Roman historians and poets portrayed them as uncouth barbarians, descended from equally barbaric ancestors who lived 'in tents, unclothed and unshod, sharing their women and bringing up all their children together', their bodies painted or tattooed with strange designs. This was all hearsay, of course, and embellished for political effect. Even the great Bede, writing his *Ecclesiastical History* in the early 8th century, repeated political propaganda fed to him by the Scots when he wrote of Picts coming by sea from Scythia to Ireland, asking for land of the Irish *Scotti* and being sent on to settle instead in northern Britain. As the Picts had come without their women, they were given Scottic wives on condition that 'when any dispute arose, they should choose a king from the female royal line rather than the male', thus neatly preparing the way for the eventual 'legitimate' takeover of Pictland by the Scots.

Worse was to come in the way of myth-building. In the 12th century, an anonymous Norwegian historian wrote: 'The Picts were little more than pygmies in stature. They worked marvels in the morning and evening building towns, but at midday they entirely lost their strength and lurked through fear in little underground houses'. This vision of tiny Picts living underground persisted into this century, colouring both Robert Louis Stevenson's ballad, 'Heather Ale', and John Buchan's story, 'No-man's land'. Folklore insists that the first Vikings who came to Rousay in Orkney dared not land because of beings like elves or trolls bearing shining spears, and even Sir Walter Scott believed that the galleries in the walls of the brochs were low and narrow because of the small size of the Picts (in common with his generation, Sir Walter mistakenly believed these prehistoric stone towers to be Pictish).

The reality about the Picts is perhaps more prosaic, but they remain a fascinating people. First their name—or rather the name by which others knew them, because we have no means of knowing what name or names they used themselves. *Picti* was first recorded in a Latin poem of AD 297, and it is thought that it may have originated as a nickname amongst the Roman garrisons of northern Britain. It is possible that at that time the Picts painted or tattooed their bodies, but no mention is made of such a custom by Bede, writing of the Picts in the later 7th and 8th centuries. The symbols on the carved stones may have begun as personal decoration in the early centuries AD and been transferred later to clothing, personal belongings and stonecarving.

A portrait of a Pict incised on a piece of slate from **Jarlshof** in Shetland.

This fine head of a Pict decorates a gilt-bronze pin found at Golspie, Sutherland (now in the Royal Museum of Scotland, Edinburgh).

Opposite
The cross-slab at **Elgin** (Moray) has an appropriate setting within the ruined cathedral but it was originally discovered during street repairs in 1823 near St Giles' Church.

There is a distinctly malevolent air about the Rhynie man, the most recently discovered of a series of carved stones found in the Rhynie area of Grampian (Gordon District). Such large-scale single figures are rare in the Pictish repertoire (this one stands fully 1.03 m high) and must surely have served a special purpose. The aura of strength and malevolence conveyed by this slightly stooping figure with its carefully drawn axe, bared teeth and hooked nose may mean that this is no ordinary portrait of a Pict but an evocation of some character from Pictish mythology. The stone is displayed in Woodhill House in Aberdeen, head-quarters of Grampian Regional Council, and there is a cast in the Royal Museum of Scotland, Edinburgh.

Could this threatening scene be a graphic expression of paganism versus Christianity? The bearded warrior with axe and knife at the ready appears to be confronting two Christian symbols: the lion that represents the Evangelist, St Mark, and the fish which is one of the earliest and most lasting of Christian motifs. Or is it simply another version of the biblical story of David fighting the lion? This is a detail of the carving on the back of a cross-slab from Golspie, Sutherland (in Dunrobin Museum).

The Picts were not a new element in the population. They were simply the descendants of indigenous iron-age tribes given a new name. From various references in the works of Roman authors, it appears that a process of tribal amalgamations took place during the Roman period; by the early 3rd century a number of smaller tribes had been absorbed into two confederations: the *Caledonii* and the *Maeatae*, and by the end of the century both were labelled *Picti*. They were a frequent harassment to the soldiers along Hadrian's Wall in the 3rd and 4th centuries, even attacking south of the Wall by coming in from the sea. Loot from some of these raids may account for the ready supplies of silver available to later Pictish craftsmen—part of a Roman silver spoon was found amongst the hoard of Pictish silverwork from Norrie's Law in Fife.

As indigenous inhabitants, the Picts had no need to beg wives from Ireland, and, although Bede claims that the Picts practised matrilinear succession in his own day, modern historians are divided over whether this was really true. Women are very rarely portrayed in Pictish art, although they could be given the special burial in formal grave-monuments accorded to the leading sector of Pictish society (see p 51). Such burials demolish the much-loved myth about the Picts being 'little more than pygmies in stature': in common with contemporary peoples in Britain, their average height was only a couple of centimetres below the modern average. The notion that they lived underground led to the mistaken identification of Tayside *souterrains*, or earth-houses, as Pictish, but these belonged to iron-age settlements and went out of use around the end of the 2nd century—and they were storehouses rather than dwellings.

If we attempt to distinguish reality from myth, we find a perfectly respectable population inhabiting the whole of the mainland and islands north of the Forth and Clyde estuaries who, from the later 3rd century, were known as Picts. Much of Argyll was lost to the Scots, whose gradual settlement of the area led by the 6th century to the establishment of the kingdom of Dalriada. Historical records of the Pictish kings also begin in the mid 6th century, and by the end of that century the conversion of the Pictish kingdom to Christianity had begun. The cultural influence of the Church was considerable for it brought Pictland into the mainstream of European art and civilisation. The emergence of the kingdom of the Picts mirrored the social developments taking place elsewhere in Britain but without the political instability created by the arrival of land-hungry Angles and

Saxons from North Germany. This internal stability provided ideal conditions for the development of Pictish art and stonecarving. There were inter-tribal problems among the Picts from time to time, as well as political and territorial struggles with their neighbours, particularly the Scots to the west and the Angles to the southeast. The independent kingdom of the Picts came to an end in the 9th century; their distinctive culture was gradually replaced in the far north by Scandinavian ideas and elsewhere Pictland became Scotland.

The only Pictish documents to have survived are copies of lists of kings, written in Latin. There are no monastic annals, records of events year by year, such as those kept by monks on Iona, in Ireland and in England. Yet it is inconceivable that monasteries in Pictland were idle in this respect and wrote nothing. We know from Bede that messengers were sent from the Pictish king, Nechton, to Ceolfrid, abbot of the twin Northumbrian monasteries of Monkwearmouth and Jarrow, in AD 710, asking for advice on Church matters. It has been argued that the letter was written for Nechton by an Englishman at his court named Egbert, rather than by a Pictish scribe; nevertheless, when Ceolfrid's reply arrived, the advice that it contained was 'immediately sent out under a public order to all the provinces of the Picts to be copied, learned, and adopted', and this can only have been done in Pictish monasteries. We can only speculate about the other manuscripts of Pictland, although a strong case has been made for allowing the possibility that the illustrated gospels known as the Book of Kells was created in a monastery somewhere in eastern Pictland. The stylistic links between the Book of Kells and Pictish stonecarving are certainly very impressive. If such documents were being produced in Pictland, what happened to them? Some may have been destroyed after the Scots took over—any Pictish annals might have been suppressed then for political reasons—and the rest may have fallen foul of reforming zeal in the 16th century.

A few Latin inscriptions carved on stone have survived from the 8th and 9th centuries, and the fact that the inscriptions on one of the sword-fittings in the St Ninian's Isle treasure are written in Latin (see p 44) suggests that knowledge of the language was not confined to the Church by the later 8th century. Earlier, however, there were clearly language problems: Ceolfrid's letter in the early 8th century had to be translated for the Pictish king and his 'learned men', from Latin into the Pictish dialect of Celtic. This dialect was not the same as Gaelic, the Celtic language spoken in Ireland; thus St Columba had needed the help of interpreters when he was in Pictland in the later 6th century.

The lack of Pictish manuscripts means that we are dependent for information upon records kept outside Pictland and upon the evidence of archaeology and art-history.

Were massive silver chains the emblems of royal office? Made of solid silver and weighing more than 2 kg, this ceremonial chain bears a double disc and Z-rod symbol, inlaid with red enamel, on its fastening ring (nine other such chains have survived; this one is in the Royal Museum of Scotland, Edinburgh).

The excitement of re-discovery — the cross-slab at St Madoes (Perth and Kinross) has been hidden within a protective wooden box for some years, but the box was removed for one day in 1988 so that the stone could be properly recorded by draughtsmen from the Royal Commission on the Ancient and Historical Monuments of Scotland.

Papil, Shetland: the design of this cross-slab has a pleasing simplicity. The lion is the Evangelist's symbol of St Mark, but the strange bird-men below may be a later addition to the stone.

The earliest carved stones are those on which Pictish symbols are incised directly into the natural, unshaped surface of the stone (symbol stones; sometimes known as Class I), and these were gradually replaced in technique and design by symbol-bearing cross-slabs (Class II), carved in relief as well as incision on carefully dressed slabs with the Christian cross as a dominant motif. Both are found in eastern and northern Scotland, but symbol stones are more prolific in Grampian and around the Moray Firth (with scattered examples in western Scotland), whereas cross-slabs are concentrated in Tayside. Both symbols and various forms of cross were also carved on the walls of caves along the coasts of Fife (East Wemyss; Caiplie) and Moray (Covesea).

The fact that so many symbol-bearing stones have survived the last twelve or more centuries is itself proof of how common a sight they were in Pictish times. Some we know to have been lost or destroyed in relatively recent times: a stone at Lynchurn on Speyside survived until the late 19th century only to be re-used as a tombstone, its finely incised crescent and V-rod symbol removed. We are told in old records that 'the person who had appropriated the stone spent much labour in chipping off the whole of the pattern. The individual who committed this piece of vandalism is now buried beneath the ancient monument he so wantonly destroyed.' Resting uneasily perhaps!

In other cases, stones recorded in the 18th or 19th century have simply vanished. One of these was specially important for our knowledge of Pictish life in Shetland, where few examples of symbols have survived. In 1774 the Reverend George Low described and, fortunately, drew a sketch of a stone that he had seen at Sandness on the west

coast of mainland Shetland: it bore three incised symbols, the rectangle, the horseshoe and the mirror. Neither the Reverend Low nor the local people understood the significance of the designs, but the stone had 'a sort of superstitious value' locally, and it was undoubtedly such superstition that throughout Scotland saved many carved stones from destruction. It was surely 'superstitious value' or antiquarian interest that prompted the Baptist missionary to Shetland to adopt the famous Papil cross-slab as a somewhat unexpected tombstone for his family burial-place on the Isle of West Burra.

The exquisite craftsmanship of the Hilton of Cadboll stone is a visual testimony to the wealth and patronage available in the 8th century. The hunting scene includes a rare portrayal of a woman, here riding side-saddle (top left of the panel), and the decorative vine-scroll running down either side is typical of contemporary Northumbrian sculpture.

What is even more surprising is the extent to which individual stones have travelled from their original location, a factor that has an important limiting effect on studies of their topographical settings. Not far from the **Aberlemno** stones in Angus, another cross-slab was found in 1819 in the foundations of a tower-house at Woodwray; it was given to Sir Walter Scott, who set it up in his garden at Abbotsford in the Borders, and eventually in 1923 it was presented to the Society of Antiquaries of Scotland in Edinburgh for their museum. Its elaborately decorated cross had been chiselled off in religious fervour before it was relegated to builder's rubble for the tower-house foundations, and the same fate befell the cross on what is still one of the finest of Scotland's Dark Age sculptures, the slab found near the **Hilton of Cadboll** chapel on the coast of Easter Ross. In this case, the cross was replaced by a funerary inscription dated 1676—yet the exuberant decoration on the back of the stone was allowed to remain. In the second half of the 19th century, it was removed from Hilton of Cadboll and erected in the grounds of Invergordon Castle until 1921 when it was sent to London to the British Museum. Instant protests from Scottish antiquaries resulted in its return within the year to Edinburgh—currently it

is the centre-piece of the early medieval sculpture display in the Royal Museum of Scotland in Queen Street, Edinburgh.

Many stones were re-used and even re-shaped in antiquity, often for secular purposes. The once magnificent cross-slab, no 7, at **St Vigeans** was drastically re-shaped, perhaps in an effort to make it conform with free-standing crosses, and the symbol stone at **Abernethy** was trimmed to make a convenient building block for the foundations of a house in the village. A more aesthetic purpose was devised for the symbol stone from Lindores: set on a south-facing slope above the village, first a finely worked sundial was added to the existing symbols and later a bench-mark (after a period of being built into a garden wall in the village, this stone is now under cover at nearby Abdie churchyard).

Despite defacement, loss, displacement or even destruction, the wealth, both in number and imagery, of the surviving symbol stones is an astounding testimony to the artistry and output of Pictish sculptors. There are 16 individual symbol-bearing stones in state care, many in the open air, along with collections of stones at **Meigle, St Vigeans** and **St Andrews**, and they form an outstanding sample of Pictish stone-carving. Many other examples are illustrated in this book for comparison, several from the large collections in the Royal Museum of Scotland, Edinburgh and in the privately-owned museum at Dunrobin Castle, Sutherland.

There was, of course, more to the Picts than their symbol stones, and an attempt has been made here both to set the stones in the context of their times and to explore what the stones themselves have to say about Pictish life. Several of the domestic settlements in state care were inhabited in Pictish times, and these provide tangible evidence of houses and everyday tools. The **Burghead Well** (Moray) lies within a great Pictish fort, and the boar carved near the summit of the hill at **Dunadd** in Argyll strikes a Pictish note within a royal stronghold of the Scots of Dalriada, a mute legacy from some episode in Picto-Scottish relations.

The Picts were farmers, horse-breeders, fishermen and craftsmen, but above all they were warriors and theirs was an heroic society cast in the mould of their Celtic forebears. Their high-kings could command to battle war-lords, each with his band of warriors, travelling by land or water. One mustering centre whose feasting hall could tell many a fine tale was the royal fortress at **Burghead**.

The Lindores stone at Abdie (North-east Fife): the triple disc and crescent and V-rod symbols are overlain by a sundial and a bench-mark. There is a mirror on one side of the stone.

The Picts shared an interest in allegorical monsters with contemporary peoples throughout Europe in the 8th and 9th centuries. This fine stone at Rossie Priory (Perth and Kinross) is unusual both in bearing a cross on both sides and in the variety and detail of its monsters: the cross on this face stands out in high relief like that on the **Aberlemno** churchyard stone (see p 23) and is surrounded by wonderfully ingenious figures in low relief. The two antlered beasts bottom left each has the head of a bird in its mouth, and a foot of each bird is interlocked with the nearside foreleg of its tormentor. Above this foursome, a beast and a fish-tailed serpent have hold of an unfortunate human whose head is in the beast's mouth and whose ankle is gripped in the serpent's mouth. A bird-headed human threatens an animal with a large axe, top right, while the animal below the right arm of the cross tries to swallow a serpent already laced in and out of his own neck and belly. The intertwined creatures at bottom right have the bodies of animals, the heads of bearded men and their tails end in animal heads.

11

SPOTLIGHT ON
BURGHEAD—A GREAT PICTISH FORT

Aerial view of **Burghead.**

Burghead has a visible history that goes back more than one and a half thousand years. As you pass through its orderly grid of streets, the neat lines of houses give way to the grass-grown ramparts of a Pictish fortress and to the cavernous ancient well that served the fort's inhabitants.

The artificially regular lay-out of this village on the Moray coast is the clue to its origin as one of the newly planned settlements of 18th- and 19th-century improvement. It was built between 1805 and 1809 and, unfortunately for the archaeologist, its construction obliterated half of the largest Pictish fort known. Even the ramparts that survive are much reduced in size because they were robbed for rubble to build the harbour. Several old maps, including one made for General Roy in 1793, recorded the basic plan of the fort, and excavations in the later 19th century and in the 1960s have filled out the picture to some extent. Natural terracing at the end of the promontory was adapted to create an upper and lower enclosure within the fort, outlined by ramparts, and at least three ramparts and ditches were dug across the neck of the promontory,

Plan of **Burghead** fort.

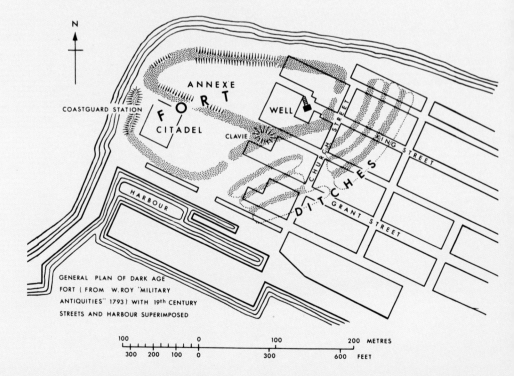

GENERAL PLAN OF DARK AGE FORT (FROM W. ROY "MILITARY ANTIQUITIES" 1793) WITH 19TH CENTURY STREETS AND HARBOUR SUPERIMPOSED

Opposite
The **Burghead** promontory was not by nature well defended but it was heightened artificially by ramparts.

12

Bull carving in the British
Museum, London.

Bull carving in Elgin
Museum.

enclosing an area of almost 3 hectares. It is possible that these three outer lines may have belonged to an earlier iron-age fort that the Picts re-used and improved. These outer defences were probably built of earth and rubble, but the inner fort was enclosed by massive walls with carefully coursed stone faces: they are shown as broad bands of collapsed stonework on a map of 1747.

It was this handy source of stone that was used to build the harbour, and there are tantalising records of the carved slabs that were found—and then built into the quay. We are told of 'mouldings and carved figures, particularly of a bull', and it is tempting to imagine the great wall of the upper ward in its heyday, embellished with carvings, and prominent among them the symbol of strength and power: the bull. Thirty bull-stones are mentioned in old records, and more may have passed unnoticed, for incised carving is easy to overlook when the lines are filled in with earth, but six have since been re-discovered during repairs and alterations to the harbour.

The bulls are virtually identical, about 400 mm long, and each is a masterpiece of carving, with glaring eyes and lowered head, muscular limbs and solid hooves—and in two cases an angrily swishing tail. Each is solitary; nothing detracts from the power image of the bull. Two remain at

Burghead in the public library on Grant Street, two are in the museum at Elgin, one is in the Royal Museum of Scotland in Edinburgh, and one is in the British Museum in London.

The bull carvings are likely to date from the 7th century (see pp 18-20) and perhaps mark a refurbishing of the fort at an important period in its history. Our dating evidence for the fort rests primarily upon radiocarbon dates; these suggest that the fort was built sometime in the period from the 4th to the 6th centuries AD and destroyed sometime in the 9th or 10th centuries. The scale of the fort and the bull-carvings imply an importance within the Pictish kingdom that is in keeping with the grandeur of the **Burghead Well**, the only part of the fort in state care.

The well is an astounding structure. It lies within the lower ward of the inner fort and, although used in medieval times and re-roofed in relatively modern times, the basic well-chamber seems to belong to the Pictish fort. One of the bull-stones is said to have been found in the well, but a record of 1862 makes it clear that this was not so. Nevertheless a Pictish origin is more likely than any other: in the past it was thought to be Roman, but there is no evidence of major Roman activity in the area. It has also been given a Christian function as a baptistry, and this is more possible, for there was a monastery close by in the 8th-10th centuries.

Glamis Manse, Angus: a great
cauldron hangs from a sturdy
frame, and the legs of two
unfortunate victims wave
helplessly from inside the
vessel. Is this an execution by
drowning or a scene from
Pictish folklore?

A flight of twenty rock-cut steps leads down towards what appears to be a huge black hole in the grassy slope—it could be the setting for Orpheus daring to enter the underworld. Once your eyes adjust to the gloom at the bottom of the steps, you find yourself at the threshold of a large square chamber cut into solid bedrock, with a platform surrounding the central tank and a basin and pedestal in opposite corners. The well looks bottomless through the dark water but in fact the tank is only 1.3 m deep.

It is difficult to tell the original work from later modifications, but it seems likely that this was always a well of imposing proportions, suited to the needs of a large community, whatever those needs may have been aside from a domestic water-supply. Given the importance of water gods to their Celtic ancestors, the pagan Picts may also have had water rituals that could have been modified and absorbed into a Christian Pictland. The traditional method of execution among the Picts was drowning, even for important political prisoners of royal blood; two such executions are recorded in the 730s, one of the victims the 'King of Atholl', the ruler of a vital strategic frontier area between the Picts and the Scots. The curious scene depicted on the cross-slab at Glamis Manse in Angus may illustrate such an execution, in which the victims were plunged headfirst into a great cauldron. It seems possible that the grandiose Burghead Well may have had a similar purpose.

It may not be entirely coincidence that Burghead should be the scene for a re-emergence in later times of a fire-festival: the Clavie, a barrel of tar on a pole, is carried burning round the village in January and brought to rest on a plinth that caps a well-preserved remnant of one of the old Pictish ramparts. This unusual survival of a tradition rooted in pagan times may reflect, however faintly, the powerful role once played by the great Pictish fort.

Excavations in the late 19th century are said to have uncovered the stone foundations of a row of buildings lining both long sides of the lower ward of the fort, with a central open space. If this is so, we can envisage the great well at one end of this open area. Disappointingly few objects have survived from the various disturbances of the fort in the last century, perhaps because, as one source admits, 'battleaxes and spearheads' were given away to tourists. The finest object to survive is particularly appropriate to a military fort: an elaborately decorated silver mount from the

mouth of a blast-horn. This is Anglo-Saxon work of the 9th century of which a Pictish war-lord could have been rightly proud.

Somewhere to the landward side of the fort was a major ecclesiastical foundation, of which the only evidence is a number of sculptured fragments including a corner-post and part of a panel from a slab-built shrine similar to the **St Andrews** Sarcophagus (see p 40; these two pieces are in the public library at Burghead). Again, the presence of an important church underlines the status of the fort, for it implies patronage, perhaps even royal patronage.

Both fort and church were destroyed, probably by the Vikings, sometime in the 9th or 10th centuries, the end of an era during which Burghead had played a dominant role in northern Pictland.

The well at **Burghead:** a flight of well-worn steps leads down into a yawning black hole. After prolonged rain the water rises to lap over the bottom steps.

The round tower at **Abernethy** (Perth and Kinross) is all that remains standing of the monastery that flourished here in the 11th century. The hill in the background is crowned by an iron-age fort that may have been re-used by the Picts.

Displayed against the wall of the tower at **Abernethy** is a symbol stone bearing the 'tuning-fork' symbol flanked by a blacksmith's hammer and anvil above a crescent and V-rod. It was dug out of the foundations of a house in the village, which accounts for the fact that it has been trimmed down to a convenient size. Several fragments of later sculptures have also been found re-used for building purposes and are now in the Royal Museum of Scotland, Edinburgh.

WHAT ARE PICTISH SYMBOLS?

T HE Picts have retained their aura of mystery mostly on account of their symbol stones. No other contemporary people in western Europe has left a comparable legacy of stonecarving, and there is no doubt that, in some respects, the Picts were unique. It is not simply the idea of using symbols that sets them apart—the Celts, the Romans, the early Christians all used symbols as a simple and graphic means of communication—but rather the way in which they used them and the extent to which they used them. They put symbols on small objects and on the walls of caves, but primarily they carved them on large stones that were set upright as a visible and important component of the Pictish landscape. Some 200 symbol stones have survived, from the Firth of Forth to the Northern and Western Isles, and new ones are discovered almost every year (usually turned up by the plough), so the total is likely to go on rising.

There is a wide variety of symbols, some of which were used more commonly than others. There are abstract designs, pictures of objects and of animals, both real animals and fantasy creatures, and sometimes these concepts are mixed in one symbol, such as the real serpent against an abstract Z-rod. But there is a problem in trying to categorise them that stems from our modern perception: what is abstract or alien to us may have been perfectly recognisable to the Picts, the Z-rod as real an object to them as the serpent. If not real, the meaning was presumably clear enough in its context. The widespread use and uniformity of the symbols imply that they were a means of communication throughout Pictland, cutting across tribal differences. The origins of many of the symbols can be traced in earlier times, among the Celtic ancestors of the Picts, and they may have retained something of their original

meanings, particularly the animal symbols. Thus the stag and the boar represent not only spirits of the forest and the importance of hunting but also prosperity and fertility in the case of the stag and battle in the case of the boar. Significantly when the boar appears in a Pictish context, it is with dorsal bristles raised for battle just as among the Celts. The serpent represents both the under-

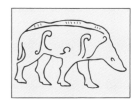

The boar at **Knocknagael** (Inverness) is a clear descendant of a Celtic power symbol, his dorsal bristles raised for battle. The stone, a massive slate boulder, is weathered and both boar and the disc and rectangle symbol above him are difficult to make out.

These two incised animals from Ardross, now in Inverness Museum and Art Gallery, were probably carved by the same hand: the treatment of the jawline and neck is identical and both show an assurance of design. Top is the beast symbol, a gentle and elegant creature, while bottom is a powerful image of a wolf.

world and healing, while the eagle, appropriately, is a sky god, a solar emblem. That aggressive bird, the goose, represents war, and the bull is a symbol of strength and ferocity. Such meanings may have been part of the symbolism for the Picts, but there must also have been a more formal element in what had become a system of symbols.

In most cases, there are two symbols on each stone, sometimes accompanied at the bottom by a mirror and comb. The latter combined symbol is often taken to represent a woman, but there is no reason to suppose that either object was particularly appropriate to a woman rather than to a man. It does, however, look as if the two top symbols make a statement together, which is sometimes qualified by the mirror and comb symbol. Several theories have been argued as to the formal meaning of the symbols and the purpose for which the stones were erected. The most widely accepted explanation is that the stones are personal memorials and that the symbols identify the status and tribe, or occasionally occupation, of the dead person. In this context the mirror and comb is often interpreted as meaning that the memorial had been commissioned by a wife or daughter. Inscribed memorial stones were certainly in use by this time outside Pictland (good examples are the Catstane, Edinburgh, and the Yarrow stone, Ettrick and Lauderdale, both 6th century in date), and the Picts may have adopted the custom even in pre-Christian contexts. There is archaeological evidence for symbol stones

This stone, known as the **Picardy Stone** (near Insch, Gordon), is a hard whinstone streaked with quartzite and appears still to be in its original location. In the mid 19th century a grave was found close to the stone and covered by stones piled round its foot. There are three incised symbols: double disc and Z-rod, serpent and Z-rod (the serpent coiling in and out of the rod) and a mirror.

having been found close to burials—the evidence is circumstantial rather than conclusive, but the many instances in which the stones appear to relate to graves are unlikely all to be coincidental, and they imply that one function at least was that of tombstone. A symbol stone was ploughed up in the Dairy Park, Dunrobin (Sutherland), and excavation of a stony patch in the vicinity uncovered a burial cairn on which the symbol stone had almost certainly been set upright as a memorial. In other cases, as at Easterton of Roseisle (Moray), the symbol stone had been used as one of the slabs forming the cist or stone coffin.

An alternative explanation arose out of the work of a social anthropologist, Anthony Jackson, using an approach that is particularly appropriate to the study of symbols and of the society reflected by them. In this light, the symbols are seen to identify lineages and the stones to be public statements of marriage alliances between lineages—and here the mirror and comb is thought to indicate the endowment paid by one lineage to the other on the occasion of the marriage. This explanation is clearly not one that archaeology can prove one way or the other. Its weakness lies in the assumptions that it makes about the nature of Pictish society, themselves arguable: in particular that the Picts were matrilinear (reckoning descent through the female line). In time, perhaps, historical and archaeological evidence and anthropological theory will reach a workable compromise.

Perhaps we should not expect a single explanation to account for all symbol stones. The symbols themselves could be used in different ways and in different contexts: a symbol carved on the wall of a cave or scratched on a bone may not convey the same message as the identical symbol on a standing stone or on a piece of fine silver jewellery. Animals carved alone had a function separate from those combined with other symbols, as we have seen in the case of the **Burghead** bulls. Symbol stones are sometimes found in groups (e.g. Rhynie in Gordon), and there should be a reason for this particular location—perhaps the residence nearby of a chieftain, as is suggested below at **Aberlemno**. In other cases, there may be the impression of stones located on land boundaries, perhaps as markers, though they may also have had a funerary purpose.

What of the crucial question of dating? Until recently, there were no closely datable archaeological contexts in which symbol stones had been found, and the only clues to date lay in art-

historical analysis of the carvings. In particular, the close similarities between Pictish animals and those in the early illustrated gospel-books led to most symbol stones being given a date in the 7th century AD. Identical details of design can be seen to link Pictish eagles, for example, with the eagle symbol of the Evangelist, St John, and, although there has been some argument as to who influenced whom, there is no doubt that there was contact between Pictish sculptors and the Christian monasteries producing the manuscripts. The early symbol stones are concentrated in Grampian and around the Moray Firth, and it has been argued, on the ground that the best designed and executed symbols will be the earliest in date, that the custom of erecting symbol stones originated in the Moray Firth area in the 6th century. Such a date fits in very neatly with documentary evidence for the presence in the Inverness area of the Pictish king, Bridei son of Maelchon, when St Columba visited the royal court in AD 565. The 'best' of the Pictish eagles was found even further north in Orkney (a stone from the Knowe of Burrian, now in the Royal Museum of Scotland, Edinburgh), and it has been

argued that this was carved at an earlier date than its manuscript counterparts were painted and that it was the inspiration for the latter. Such art-historical arguments are difficult to prove, however, and the assumption that the best examples must be the earliest could conceivably be reversed.

The Craw Stane at Rhynie (Gordon) is probably still in its original position, a granite pillar on a hill-slope carved with a fish and an 'elephant'. Seven other symbol stones have been found in the vicinity, including the striking study of an axeman illustrated on p 6.

Symbols on silver: the plaques from Norrie's Law (Fife) with double disc and Z-rod and beast's head inlaid with red enamel. Each plaque is 90 mm long and there is no clue as to how they were used. (Royal Museum of Scotland, Queen Street, Edinburgh.)

At present, the earliest datable context for a symbol stone is also in Orkney. A domestic settlement at Pool on the island of Sanday yielded a stone carved with a double-disc symbol in a level dated by scientific means to the mid 6th century. The **Burghead** bulls could be as early, but it cannot be proved that they were contemporary with the building of the fort (they could have been carved on the walls at a later date); the scrolls with which the stonecarver has indicated the leg muscles of the bulls are so similar to those in 7th-century manuscripts that they are usually assigned to the same period. There may be a missing piece of the chronological jigsaw, if symbols carved or painted on wooden planks preceded symbol stones proper.

If we consider the equipment needed by the stone-carvers, relatively few tools are involved: hammer, punch and chisel of tempered (hardened) iron for the initial carving, and a selection of smoothing tools made of a stone harder than the slab being worked on. Close examination of incised lines on symbol stones shows that the design was first laid out by individual dots or pits, pocked by hammer

and punch, and then the pits were linked by pocking a continuous groove. A practical experiment in producing the sort of groove seen on symbol stones (most are 3-5 mm deep and 11-18 mm or more wide) demonstrated that the pocking process is quick, a hammer and punch producing a line 150 mm long in just a few minutes, but that the punch needed frequent sharpening. Smoothing the pocked groove was far more time-consuming, involving hours of rubbing with a pebble of suitable size and hardness.

A number of symbol stones bear inscriptions carved in the simple linear lettering known as ogam (or ogham). Ogam was invented in Ireland sometime before AD 400 and seems to have been introduced into Pictland by the 7th century by Irish missionaries. Its advantage was the ease with which the letters could be cut on wood or stone, and the Irish used it mostly for memorial stones. It may have been used in the same way in Pictland but, as the Pictish inscriptions are largely unintelligible, it is impossible to be certain. The individual letters can be transliterated into their equivalent Latin letters, but the result is usually a jumble of letters making very little sense, apart from a few possible personal names (e.g. Nehhton for Nechton) and possible versions of the Gaelic word *mac*, meaning 'son of' (e.g. *maqq* or *meqq*). Ogam occurs on symbol stones, cross-slabs and plain slabs, but on symbol stones and cross-slabs it can often look very much an afterthought—almost a footnote. Whatever the message, it seems unlikely to have repeated the message of the symbols themselves. Ogam was also used on small objects (see p 48). It seems to have been used intermittently from the 7th to 10th centuries, mostly in northern Pictland (21 of the 37 known inscriptions originate north of the Moray Firth).

If most symbol stones belong to the 6th and 7th centuries, they were created at a time when Christianity was gradually spreading amongst the Picts. Eventually the Christian message was displayed on cross-slabs, alongside the Pictish symbols and in some cases, such as **Dyce** and **Aberlemno**, in the same locations.

The old church of St Fergus at **Dyce**, Aberdeen, is now an ivy-clad ruin, and the carved stones, believed to have been found in the vicinity, are displayed in an alcove built into the outside of the east gable-wall. The earliest is a symbol stone incised with a pair of symbols: a swimming elephant above a double disc and Z-rod, each disc embellished with an inner circle and central dot. The cross-slab is also a granite slab carved on one

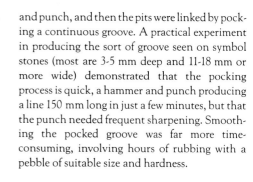

The smooth surface and fine texture of this stone from Dunrobin allowed the stone-carver to achieve cleanly incised lines and decorative details such as the ornament along the central plate of the comb and on the handle of the 'tuning fork' (Sutherland; Dunrobin Castle Museum).

The symbol stone at **Brandsbutt,** Inverurie, has suffered rough-handling in the past; it was found in several fragments built into an adjacent stone dyke and, although still incomplete, it was clearly once a fine large slab of whinstone. There are two symbols, a crescent and V-rod above a serpent and Z-rod, and the head of the serpent and the markings on its body are particularly well drawn. Running up the left-hand side of the stone and originally vertical is a fine ogam inscription, which reads IRATADDOARENS.

The top of this slab from Ackergill (Caithness) has been damaged but the belly and fins of a fish are visible, above a rectangle and an ogam inscription (Royal Museum of Scotland, Edinburgh).

side only, and both have at some time in the past been trimmed down from their original size. The cross is boldly sculpted in relief, entirely filled with interlace within a plain moulded frame. Clustering round the foot of the cross are four symbols: the crescent and V-rod, the disc and rectangle, the triple ring or cauldron symbol and the double-disc and Z-rod, all elaborately decorated.

Below the symbol stone and cross-slab are two small carved fragments, one of which (on the right beneath the cross-slab) could be part of a corner-post from a slab-built shrine. Two cross-incised grave-markers are mounted on the side-walls of the alcove. As a group, these stones span the 6th to 9th centuries, beginning with the symbol stone.

Opposite
The high relief of the cross on the churchyard stone involved hours of work in chipping away the unwanted rock.

The stones at Aberlemno, near Forfar (Angus), are a perfect introduction to the range and skill of Pictish craftsmen. The three stones—one symbol stone and two cross-slabs—span the 6th to early 9th centuries. They demonstrate incised carving and relief sculpting, and they range in subject across symbolism, secular story-telling and Christian iconography.

The symbol stone and the later of the two cross-slabs stand beside the modern road (Forfar to Brechin); the cross-slab is still in its original stone base, and the symbol stone was moved here from the adjacent field. (The third stone beside the road was also shifted here from the field: it bears faint traces of a crescent and a curving line and may either be an unfinished symbol stone or a relatively modern fake and will not be mentioned again.) The second cross-slab now stands in the churchyard downslope to the south, but this is not an early church-site and the stone is likely to have stood closer to the other two when first erected. At least two other carved stones are known to have been found nearby: a symbol stone bearing an arch or horseshoe symbol above an 'elephant', which was turned up by the plough on Flemington Farm, Aberlemno, a little to the east, and a symbol-bearing cross-slab built into the foundations of a tower-house at Woodwray, just north of Aberlemno.

In reconstructing the Pictish landscape, we must consider at least two symbol stones and three cross-slabs as a group that was set up on the ridge of land between the South Esk and Lunan valleys. Why should this particular place have qualified for such memorials? A ridge between two valleys could have acted as a territorial boundary. On the twin hills to the immediate west are the iron-age forts of Finavon and Turin, and a good case has been argued for a re-building of the defences of the Finavon fort in early historic times. If this were an important power centre, the Aberlemno stones would be a significant part of the contemporary landscape in relation to the fort.

Of the three carved stones in state care at Aberlemno, the earliest is the naturally-shaped pillar stone, now tilted at an angle, on which a serpent, a double disc and Z-rod and a mirror and comb were incised, probably in the 6th or 7th century. There are prehistoric cupmarks carved low down on the other side, which suggests that the Picts may have taken advantage of an existing standing stone.

A century or so later, the cross-slab now in Aberlemno churchyard was erected. This is a superb piece of carving and an extraordinarily satisfying visual achievement. It stands 2.3 m high and has been carefully shaped so that it tapers towards its triangular top; from an original thickness of some 300 mm the background to the cross has been dressed down with painstaking care so that the cross appears almost freestanding, its surface almost 100 mm proud of the rest of the slab.

Right
The symbols are so deeply incised that they appear almost in relief.

Far right
There are just two animals in this great knot of limbs: the easiest way to unravel them is to begin with their heads in the centre of each spiral and work back along their bodies. Each has an elongated snout or beak that crosses the spiral diagonally and a long ear or crest. Its body spirals round and down the spiralling body of its partner, and its foreleg and hindleg are intermeshed in each spiral respectively.

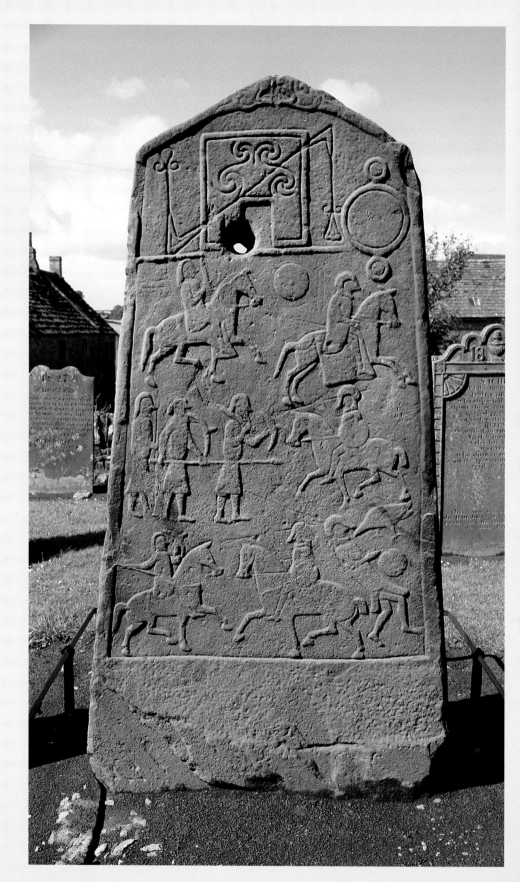

The back of the churchyard
stone has been described as a
tapestry in stone. Framed
beneath the heads of two
snarling beasts are the
indented rectangle with Z-rod
and the triple disc symbols,
while below those an action-
packed battle scene presents
a unique visual document.
The hole is not original.

24

The cross is decorated with beautifully proportioned interlace and spiral designs, while its backcloth seems alive with twining animals. The back of the slab carries two large symbols and the only large-scale battle scene known on a symbol stone, implying a special importance for the battle and, perhaps, a particular reason for its depiction here at Aberlemno. The scene should be read like a strip cartoon in three rows from top left to bottom right, and the two forces are clearly identifiable: bareheaded warriors on the left and helmeted warriors on the right. In the first strip, a warrior on horseback with his sword raised chases another horseman wearing a helmet but weaponless. In the second strip, three foot-soldiers confront a helmeted and armed warrior on horseback. The third strip shows two horsemen fighting, and, on the right, the unmistakeable conclusion to the battle: a dead warrior wearing helmet and mail tunic, carved over-large to underline his importance, lies prey for a carrion bird. 'Prey for ravens' was a poetic term for death on the battlefield; in the heroic poem, *The Gododdin*, thought to have been written about AD 600, a warrior is described as 'an uproar on the battle slope, he was a fire, his spears were impetuous, were flashing; he was the food of ravens, he was prey for ravens . . .'.

Could the Aberlemno scene be showing us a real battle? If so, who are the warriors?

Some 10 km south of Aberlemno, near the modern village of Dunnichen, a great battle took place in AD 685. Known as the Battle of Nechtansmere, this was a decisive victory for the Picts over the Angles of Northumbria, who had forcibly occupied the southern part of Pictland for the previous thirty years and who, after their defeat, were never again a power in lands north of the Forth. It has been argued, very plausibly, that this is the battle portrayed at Aberlemno. The stone was carved perhaps a century after the battle, but the folk memory of what happened on the 20th May, AD 685, and its long-term effects would still have been a vital national issue. There is even archaeological support for this identification, in that helmets with long nose-guards like those shown on the stone as worn by one of the opposing forces are known to have existed among the Anglo-Saxons. The Anglian helmet discovered in the Coppergate excavation in York is precisely this type of helmet and dates from the 8th century, contemporary with the Aberlemno stone whose sculptor would depict the Anglian foe in the manner familiar to him.

The horseman fleeing towards the right has lost or flung away his round shield, sword and spear. The handgrip of the sword, 'floating' at the rider's back, shows the shape of the pommel and guard.

This trio of foot-soldiers may tell us something of battle tactics: the front man has his shield (seen in profile) at the ready and his sword poised to slash, while the man behind grasps his spear with both hands like a lance so that it has the effect of covering the warrior in the front row. The third warrior waits with spear held at rest until needed. Even the straps are shown by which the middle warrior's shield hangs from his shoulder.

The bareheaded Pictish warrior on his long-tailed horse contrasts with the helmeted Anglian on his cropped-tail mount. The Anglian has drawn back his horse's head using the bridle to steady him and has his spear at the point of throwing, while the Pict has raised his shield in readiness to ward off the blow and is preparing to hurl his own spear, and his horse, by necessity, is running unchecked.

The end of the battle — the helmeted Anglian lies dead at the mercy of a carrion bird.

25

The cross-slab at the roadside at **Aberlemno:** the great cross-head is sculpted with raised circular and rectangular bosses, like a jewelled metal cross translated into stone. Angels carrying books adore the cross on either side.

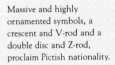

Massive and highly
ornamented symbols, a
crescent and V-rod and a
double disc and Z-rod,
proclaim Pictish nationality.

Bede records the battle: Ecgfrith, king of
Northumbria, 'rashly led an army to ravage the
province of the Picts. The enemy pretended to
retreat, and lured the king into narrow mountain
passes, where he was killed with the greater part of
his forces . . .'. The weaponless but helmeted
horseman being chased in the top strip of the
scene could be the unfortunate King Ecgfrith,
lured into an impossible situation from which he
fled, attempted to turn and make a stand with his
army (second and third strips) but was finally
killed. 'Many of the English at this time were
killed, enslaved, or forced to flee from Pictish
territory.'

By the early 9th century, the Picts had other
problems: the growing power of the Scots in their
midst. This may account for the huge, nationalistic symbols dominating the back of the other
cross-slab at Aberlemno, still standing in its
original stone socket beside the modern road (and
probably beside an ancient trackway leading from
the fort of Finavon towards the monastery at
Brechin). A cairn of stones was recorded beside it
in the 16th century, when it was considered to be
'curiouslie wrocht' or curiously wrought. It stands
almost 3 m high and is decorated not just front
and back but also on the narrow sides, and the
motifs are far more overtly Christian than any-
thing on the churchyard slab apart from the cross
itself. The carving is entirely in relief, and the
combined effects of roadside pollution and
weather erosion have blurred what must once
have been a startling monument, a commanding
wayside prayer station, commissioned by some
secular chieftain to glorify both the Christian
God and the waning kingdom of the Picts.

The hunt in full swing,
horsemen, hounds and stags.
Tucked in on the left is the
figure of David the warrior
with his square shield, and
the two trumpeters top right
are another David image, this
time as a musician.

On the right, David is
portrayed grasping the jaws of
the lion, and the sheep and
the harp symbolise his
attributes as shepherd and
musician. The splendid
centaur on the left carries a
branch of a tree that fills an
unwanted space.

There is a neat precision about the cross-slab at **Dunfallandy** (Perth and Kinross). Both front and back have a moulded frame, and the shapely cross is flanked by an ordered procession of figures. The relief outline of the cross and the bosses carved on its arms make it stand out — but why did someone, at some period in the past, chisel away the decoration in the centre panel? From the traces left, it looks as if there was once a handsome roundel filling the square frame. The slab is now protected inside a glazed shelter; although not in its original position, it seems always to have been in the vicinity of Dunfallandy House.

IMPACT OF CHRISTIANITY

THE ART OF PICTISH CROSS-SLABS

THERE had been Christians south of the Clyde and Forth estuaries since late Roman times. St Ninian took up residence as bishop amongst a Christian community at **Whithorn** in Galloway in the late 5th century, and there are inscribed Christian memorial stones surviving not only from the Whithorn area but also from around Peebles to demonstrate the lasting impact of Christian teaching. Bede, writing about AD 731, believed that St Ninian's influence had also converted the southern half of the Picts, those living south of 'a range of steep and desolate mountains' now known as the Grampian mountains. Bede is normally quite reliable, but in this instance the lack of supporting archaeological evidence suggests that the sources of his information led him to exaggerate the extent to which Christianity had gained followers north of the Forth before about AD 600.

Nowadays the credit for converting the Pictish kingdom as a whole is given to the missionaries who followed in the footsteps of St Columba. Columba (or Colum Cille) was an Irish priest, born around AD 521 in Co. Donegal, who crossed the Irish Sea with a small band of companions, having decided, in his early forties, to become 'a pilgrim for Christ'. This was in 563, and the small monastic community that he founded on the island of Iona was to become one of the most famous in Scotland. Columba's biographer, the Irish monk Adomnan, writing little more than a century later, records several journeys into Pictland. Although Adomnan describes the conversion of individual Picts, there was clearly no wholesale conversion of the Picts during Columba's lifetime; rather it was a gradual process begun by Columba and completed by later monks working both from Iona and from other monasteries as they came to be established.

Columba visited the court of the Pictish king, Bridei (or Brude) son of Maelchon, on more than one occasion, and we are told that Bridei 'greatly honoured the holy and venerable man, as was fitting, with high esteem'. Adomnan does not claim that Columba converted the king himself.

The gradual conversion of the Picts and the spread of Columban monasteries throughout Pictland had been achieved before the end of the 7th century. By AD 710 royal patronage of the church and interest in its activities was such that the

Dunfallandy: two animals form the frame, their heads carved in relief at the top and their bodies dwindling towards incised fish-tails at the bottom. No fewer than eight Pictish and one Christian (a small free-standing cross) symbol have been fitted into the design, including the blacksmith's tools of hammer, anvil and tongs.

Pictish king, Nechton, sought advice on ecclesiastical matters from the abbot of Monkwearmouth and Jarrow, and requested that Northumbrian masons be sent to Pictland to build a stone church. Previously churches had been built of timber in Irish style rather than of dressed stone as was the custom south of the Forth and Clyde.

Northumbrian influence was not new to Pictland. Northumbrian political exiles had sought refuge among the Picts in the early 7th century, one of them marrying a Pictish princess and fathering a future king, and for a period of some 17 years the most southerly part of Pictland was under Northumbrian rule until the occupying forces were defeated by the Picts at the Battle of Nechtansmere in AD 685. A Northumbrian bishopric had been created for the occupied area only four years previously, but Bishop Trumwine's residence at Abercorn, on the southern shore of the Forth, was shortlived, as he and his monks were forced to flee in the wake of the defeated Northumbrian army.

However patchy, there was thus a long-standing familiarity with Northumbrian culture by the time that Nechton asked for spiritual and practical guidance from the Northumbrian church. As we have already seen in the last chapter, the benefits of this familiarity were not necessarily all on the Pictish side, and the links between Pictish stone-carvers and Northumbrian book-painters that are detectable on symbol stones become even

stronger on cross-slabs. The idea of using symbols clearly began in pagan times, but it was not in conflict with the Christian message and symbols continued to be an important part of the design alongside the Christian cross.

Typically, the Picts made the cross-slab an art-form of their own. Instead of carving free-standing crosses like the Northumbrians and the Irish, Pictish sculptors created a cross against the backcloth of an almost rectangular slab, thereby doubling the surface area of the stone available for decoration. The reason for this, apart from the Pictish love of designs, was probably historical: the Picts had a long tradition of stone-carving, whereas for the Northumbrians and Irish it was a relatively new craft stimulated by the Church and based initially on plain wooden and stone crosses. It has also been suggested that the slab-shape may have been chosen in order to avoid placing the symbols on the cross itself. Certainly the shape gave great scope for decoration, and in the hands of a master craftsman could resemble a page from an illuminated gospel-book transferred to stone.

Cross-slabs are normally decorated on both sides, so that there is a cross-face and a back to the stone, and there may be carving along the narrow edges of the slab as well. They were clearly designed to be free-standing monuments, and they were probably prayer-crosses, placed beside tracks or on boundaries as a focus for devotion. Some were close to early church sites and may have stood within or at the entrance to monastic enclosures, while others may imply the former presence nearby of an important chieftain's residence. In some cases graves have been found close to the stone, but it is not clear whether the stone was originally set up to mark a cemetery or whether it became an appropriate place for later burials. The transport and erection of these slabs, especially the larger examples, must have posed problems in protecting the ornamented surfaces, and they are unlikely to have been carved far from their destination. The stone-carvers themselves may have travelled—a master craftsman might well be in demand over a large area—but there is also some evidence of local schools of sculpture. Some slabs, like prehistoric standing stones, were simply levered into prepared holes in the ground and their bases chocked round tightly with boulders and earth to keep them upright; others were inserted into slots in large stone blocks, like the roadside cross-slab at **Aberlemno**.

The earliest Pictish cross-slabs belong to the 8th century and, with their relief carving and decoration, they are quite distinct from the simple cross-marked stones used to locate Christian graves from the very beginnings of missionary activity. A large number of such grave-markers survives on Iona from the 6th century onwards, and in central, eastern and northern Scotland similar stones demonstrate the persistent activities of Irish missionaries among the Picts. The adoption of the large decorated cross-slab happened at roughly the same time as the Northumbrians began to sculpt large free-standing decorated crosses, and these parallel developments were undoubtedly related. Bede is our prime source of information for the events following Nechton's overture to the Northumbrians, and it is clear that the Church in Pictland and the Church in Northumbria became closer in customs and ideas at the expense of the older Columban Church. The masons dispatched from Monkwearmouth and Jarrow to the court of the Pictish king soon after AD 710 would have been impressed by the skill and technology of stone-carvers there, for their own traditions of stone sculpture dated no further back than the late 7th century, when plain crosses and a few architectural pieces were produced.

Glamis Manse (Angus), possibly the earliest of surviving cross-slabs.

The long tradition of Pictish decorative carving shows itself in the early cross-slabs. At his most skilful, the stoneworker combined the delicacy of incision with the visual impact of sculpture in relief, as we have seen already at **Aberlemno** on the churchyard stone. The cross-slab at Glamis in Angus, in the garden of the manse beside the church, could be an earlier product of the same workshop. It has the same elegant, slightly tapering shape with a triangular head, and there is the same pleasing balance of cross and background motifs. This is one of several cross-slabs that

appear to show re-use of an earlier symbol stone, for on the back of the slab, where the surface has not been dressed smooth as was the front, there are just three symbols (serpent, fish and mirror). The fact that these were not obliterated and the surface re-worked implies that they, and their monument, were still important to the community.

There is also a sense of experimentation about the Glamis stone, experiment with laying out the design and with carving techniques. The two

Far left
The cross-slab at **Elgin** (Moray): despite the difficulties of carving hard granite, the design is complex, with portraits of the evangelists flanking the cross (St John's eagle is just visible behind him, middle right, with wings outstretched) and entwined animals below the base of the cross.

Left
A modern stonemason at work carving a new decorative piece for **Elgin Cathedral**.

A medieval stonemason at work: part of a reconstructed scene in the Great Hall at **Stirling Castle**. Note the stonemason's mallet, a specialised type of hammer.

symbols to the right of the cross, a beast's head and a triple disc, are outlined by incised lines so deep as to create an impression of relief, while the figures to the left are carved partially in true low relief: the background surface of the stone has been lowered so as to leave their bodies from shoulder height down in relief. The cross itself is carved in higher relief. There seems to have been an intention to create the effect of a ring between the arms of the cross, partly by relief and partly by incision, but its completion was thwarted by the placing of the beast's head (lower right).

It is difficult to estimate the time and labour that went into the creation of a cross-slab. Skill and experience were needed, from knowing how different types of stone will fracture to understanding how to transfer designs on to stone and how to adjust the scale of the design. The process would begin with choosing the stone and quarrying it if necessary, and roughly dressing it to shape. The next task, after transporting the slab to the stonemason's workshop, would be to prepare the surface of the stone: making it smooth and level,

marking the outline of the cross and lowering the surface round the cross, leaving a frame along the edge of the slab if desired. The details of the overall design and the various levels of relief would have to be worked out carefully and their outlines marked on the slab, before the carving itself could begin. It seems logical that the cross might be carved first, as the dominant element in the design, but it may be that more than one craftsman might work on different areas of the stone at the same time. The carving finished and the slab set up at the chosen place, the final work, at least on the later cross-slabs, may well have belonged to the painters. Although no traces of paint have been found on Pictish stones, contemporary sculpture in Northumbria was certainly painted—fragments found in excavation show red paint over a white undercoat—and the Picts may have done the same.

The sculptor would need the same basic equipment and use the same basic techniques of pocking and smoothing as the earlier carver of incised symbols (see p 20), but the creation of high relief sculpture, removing substantial amounts of stone from the slab, would be both laborious and hard on his tools. The master sculptors responsible for laying out the designs must have had pattern-books, presumably painted on vellum (treated animal hide), as well as specialised tools such as dividers and compasses for transferring the designs on to the stone.

Shandwick (Ross and Cromarty): a detail of the superb spiral-filled panel on the back of the cross-slab.

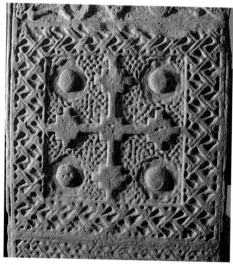

The different levels of relief and the intricacy of the carving on this panel from the Rosemarkie cross-slab underline the skills needed to plan and carry out such designs (in Groam House Museum, Rosemarkie, Ross and Cromarty).

Dunkeld Cathedral: an unfinished piece of architectural carving found originally in the grounds of Dunkeld House. At one end of the panel is a man riding bareback on a horse, holding in his right hand a spear apparently resting across his lap and in his left hand a curving blast-horn against his lips. The carving may have been intended as part of a hunting scene. Other later sculptures include a hogback gravestone (in the tower) and part of a cross-slab carved in relief with figures and animals (in the chapter house).

The stone inside the church at Nigg (Ross and Cromarty) is an extraordinary testimony to the skill of its creator. Its decoration is a superb blend of high and low relief, its use of raised bosses is restrained and effective and the detail of its carving is astounding. The group of three stones along this stretch of coastline—Hilton of Cadboll, Shandwick and Nigg—is an interesting one, each stone inter-related in a sequence of art-styles and technical development that began in the 8th century and continued into the 9th. Nigg stands central in the sequence, the wide decorative frame and low relief figural carving on the back relating it to Hilton of Cadboll, while the use of bosses on the Shandwick stone is a far less successful copy of the Nigg bosses. It is now generally accepted that the Nigg style of sculpture was a dominant influence on the decoration of St John's and St Oran's crosses on Iona, to the extent that Pictish stonecarvers may have been sent to Iona to work on the crosses. What characterises their work is the prominent boss, covered in interlace decoration and encircled by snakes. The overall design of Nigg, front and back, shows an orderly and symmetrical balancing of panels of decoration, and this use of panels becomes a distinctive feature of later cross-slabs.

Many of these magnificent cross-slabs must have belonged to contemporary churches and monasteries, and some at least of these churches may have been built of stone rather than timber, yet none survives above ground-level. Nechton's request for Northumbrian masons to build a stone church in the early 8th century has long been associated with **Restenneth Priory**, near Forfar, because of archaic features about the masonry at the base of the tower, but modern opinion prefers a late 11th-century date. Survivals of earlier buildings are fragments of sculpture: decorative panels, wall friezes and even, from Forteviot in Perthshire, the greater part of an ornamental arch (now displayed, appropriately, over the entrance to the Dark Age sculpture room in the Royal Museum of Scotland, Edinburgh). There are architectural fragments in the museums at **Meigle** (no 22; see p 61) and **St Vigeans** (no 8), in the tower at the west end of **Dunkeld Cathedral** (Perth and Kinross), and in **Dunblane Cathedral** (Stirling).

The collection of stones at **St Vigeans**, near Arbroath in Angus, implies the existence there of an early church or monastery. The stones are now displayed in a converted cottage, but they were found in the graveyard or built into the walls of the church on the steep-sided knoll that is such a

Nigg (Ross and Cromarty): much of the interlace decorating the cross proves on close inspection to be intertwining elongated animals. The bowed figures of St Paul and St Anthony fill the triangular panel at the top, with the raven holding their loaf of bread between them.

remarkable feature of the village. The church has had a long history of rebuilding, and it replaced, in medieval times, an even earlier foundation of which no trace remains except the name and the carved stones. St Vigianus was a 7th-century Irish monk, but none of the stones can be dated earlier than the 8th century, so it seems likely that the church was founded by one of his followers during that century.

Hilton of Cadboll (Ross and Cromarty): within the fenced enclosure are the grass-grown foundations of a small medieval chapel. A few kilometres to the south stands the Shandwick stone, near the site of another, long vanished, chapel, and to the south again the stone at Nigg marks a third.

The reconstructed 9th-century cross-slab, **St Vigeans** no. 1, its elegant interlace cross flanked by a medley of twining animals.

Far right
St Vigeans no. 1, back: beneath a fragment of a hunting scene are carved symbols (double disc and Z-rod, crescent, mirror and comb) and a series of scenes involving animals.

Despite the misuse that they have suffered, the stones still have a crispness of carving that shows a wealth of interesting detail. No 1 is often known as the Drosten Stone, because it has an inscription commemorating three people: Drosten, Uoret and Forcus; the four lines of this inscription are neatly carved and yet only half-fill the panel, and one wonders whether there was an intention to add more. The panel was placed at the base of one side of the slab, clearly designed to be read by people on their knees, praying before the cross. This slab was probably carved in the early 9th century. The back is crammed with symbols and busy scenes that bear no relation to one another but individually must have conveyed a lot of information to their contemporary audience: a bear lumbers along, a young deer suckles at its mother, an eagle gorges itself on a fish and an archer prepares to shoot at an advancing wild boar.

The 9th century was a time of change in Pictland, and the inscription on this stone is an appropriate reflection of the increasing ethnic and cultural mixture in the population. Drosten and Uoret are Pictish names but Forcus is Gaelic; the lettering and the word *ett* for 'and' are derived from the Latin culture of the Church, whereas *ipe* must be a Pictish word, presumably meaning 'son of' or 'nephew of'.

Cross-slab no 7 has suffered very badly, perhaps in medieval times, by being cut down so that the cross could be re-used as a grave-stone; it was probably intended that the lower part of the stone should be hidden beneath ground. The decoration on the back of the slab has been obliterated. This was an exceptionally beautiful cross, bearing a variety of intricate interlaced patterns including, on the lower half of the cross-shaft, a threefold spiral design in which each element ends in the head of a bird, a man or an animal. Apart from the two overtly Christian motifs illustrated in detail here, there are also two curious scenes: a man being held upside down over a rectangular object,

and a calf either being sacrificed or, given the emaciated little figure crouched below with his tongue sticking out, being blood-let for sustenance.

It is sometimes difficult to separate what is purely Pictish from what may be a Pictish borrowing from elsewhere, particularly from Christian iconography. Did the eagle and the fish have an independent existence as Pictish symbols or were they adopted from the equivalent Christian symbols? There can be no doubt when a motif matches up with stories familiar both from the Bible and from contemporary sculpture in Ireland, Northumbria and further south in England. Favourite themes from Christian iconography centre on David, followed closely by St Paul and St Anthony (e.g. **St Vigeans** no 7; Nigg, see p 35), Daniel in the lions' den (e.g. **Meigle** no 2, see p 58) and Jonah and the whale (e.g. **Dunfallandy**). Among the frequent portrayals of David, the most popular motif is David fighting the lion, and often the sculptor makes the identification clearer still by placing a sheep and a harp alongside to represent David the shepherd and David the musician or psalmist. David is also portrayed separately as a harpist and as a warrior. The most important surviving pieces of David-inspired sculpture are the **St Andrews** Sarcophagus (see p 40) and the cross-slabs from **Aberlemno** (see p 27) and Nigg, and as a group they demonstrate considerable interest in the biblical stories about David in the Pictland of the 8th century.

St Vigeans no. 11, back: two barefoot clerics sit side by side on a high-backed bench, while below them an enigmatic hooded figure wearing short baggy trousers confronts a second (damaged) figure, each carrying a stout and heavily knobbed stave.

Far left

St Vigeans no. 1, side: a panel has been created at the foot of the interlace decoration to display an inscription, perhaps unfinished, that reads 'Drosten ipe Uoret ett Forcus'.

The re-shaped cross-slab, no. 7, at **St Vigeans**.

The River Tay has played a special part in the early history of the church in Scotland, for it links the three most important episcopal centres first of Pictland and then of Scotland in the 8th to the 10th centuries. **Abernethy** held supreme position in 8th-century Pictland, relinquishing that role to **Dunkeld** further up the Tay after the union of the Picts and Scots in the mid 9th century; **Dunkeld** in its turn gave way to **St Andrews** on the coast of Fife south of the Tay estuary by the early 10th century. A certain amount of stone carving survives at **Abernethy** (see p 16) and **Dunkeld** (see p 34) to testify to the patronage of the Church, but the magnificent sculptures at **St Andrews**, known then as Kilremont, convey more clearly the influence of the Church in stimulating the natural skills and tastes among the Picts for creating carved stone monuments.

There was certainly a monastery at St Andrews in the first half of the 8th century, because the death of its abbot was recorded in AD 747, yet there is no stone-carving in the great collection in the Cathedral Museum that can be dated earlier than the second half of the 8th century. Monasteries were usually founded in places already important to Church or king, but there are no symbol stones to suggest that St Andrews was a centre of Pictish activities before the 8th century. In fact there are relatively few carvings of symbols surviving from Fife generally. The most important sculpture at St Andrews is the Sarcophagus, which was undoubtedly created by a sculptor working in the Pictish style but which belongs to a European tradition of Christian art and church furniture.

A major monastery such as this would have had a *scriptorium* or writing room in which the monks copied and illustrated the gospel-books. No manuscript has survived that can with certainty be hailed as the product of a Pictish monastery, perhaps because so many church treasures were lost at the Reformation, but it has been argued

Opposite:

St Andrews Cathedral and St Rule's Tower.

The **St Andrews** Sarcophagus (reconstructed).

The surviving panels and corner-posts of the **St Andrews** Sarcophagus are skilfully decorated in high relief. The long panel shows no fewer than three images of David, based on the Old Testament story: the scene is dominated by the large figure on the right, depicting David fighting the lion, both hands on the lion's jaws. The monkey carved above David's left shoulder is echoed by the pairs of monkeys on the end panel. The horseman to the left of the main David figure also represents David fighting the lion, this time with the lion leaping up to claw at the horse's neck while David holds a sword ready to strike. The falcon riding on David's left arm underlines his royal status. Below the horseman another figure of David, armed as a warrior with spear and shield, walks behind two animals with a dog at his feet, while behind him a griffin, a creature half-eagle half-lion, is savaging a mule.

that the Book of Kells may have originated in eastern Scotland—many of its beautiful illustrations are certainly very close in style to the designs on Pictish stones. The sculptor of the Sarcophagus had a familiarity with Christian iconography, and with exotic animals such as the monkeys, that suggests that he had access to illuminated books and perhaps imported art objects from Europe and beyond.

The Book of Kells is likely to have been written and illustrated sometime in the last few decades of the 8th century, and it could well have been the work of a monastic *scriptorium* at St Andrews. No trace has yet been identified of any of the buildings belonging to this early monastery.

The Sarcophagus was a chance discovery entirely dependent upon an unusually deep grave having been dug at just the right spot, and there may be other carvings locked beneath the green turf of the Cathedral precinct. Others may have been found in the past and re-used as builders' rubble—even the survival of the Sarcophagus fragments after their discovery in 1833 seems to have been a

matter of some luck. A contemporary antiquary observed 'so lightly were these priceless relics prized at the seat of the oldest University in Scotland, that for six years they lay tumbling about as if of no interest or consequence', and the same antiquary allowed them to be taken to Cupar and back in a carrier's cart so as to have casts made of them.

The Sarcophagus ranks high amongst early medieval European art and is certainly one of the most accomplished pieces of Pictish sculpture. It is an elaborate stone box consisting of corner-posts with vertical grooves into which the side-panels slot. It is in fact a shrine, created sometime in the later 8th or very early 9th century, probably to house a wooden box or reliquary containing the relics of a saint. Commissioned by the Church or by some rich lay patron, it would have been a prominent feature inside the church belonging to the great monastery that preceded both the Cathedral and St Rule's Tower. The shrine has been reconstructed from fragments found during grave-digging near the Tower in 1833; it has been given a pitched roof like a house, but it is perhaps more likely to have had a flat cover.

The Sarcophagus may originally have contained the relics of either St Rule (St Regulus) or St Andrew. According to the St Andrew's foundation legend, the church was founded in the reign of Oengus or Angus, when St Rule brought from the east the relics of St Andrew (three fingers, an arm bone, a knee cap and a tooth). This king is thought most likely to have been Angus I, who reigned in the 8th century. Whichever saint inspired the Sarcophagus, in later medieval times it was used as an ordinary coffin, for it was found with a jumble of bones almost 2 m deep in the graveyard. Perhaps it was thrown out when the chapel of St Rule was built to house St Andrew's relics in the early 11th century.

Among other sculptures in the Cathedral Museum are two fragments (nos 28 and 29) that together portray David the harpist and may be part either of the missing back panel of the Sarcophagus or of another similar slab-built shrine. A number of carved stones had been re-used by the Cathedral masons, including the great cross-shaft, no 19, and several cross-slabs, which were found built into the basal courses of the east end of the Cathedral. Despite the fact that these superbly sculpted stones were then less than 300 years old and part of the heritage of Scotland's premier diocese, they were relegated to little more than builders' rubble when the new Cathedral was begun around AD 1160.

Free-standing crosses, such as this elaborately sculpted example at **St Andrews** (no. 19), would originally have stood at strategic points in the open air within the monastic complex. Often decorated with biblical scenes, they have been described as 'sermons in stone'.

Far left
This cross-slab at **St Andrews** (no. 24) was built into the foundations of the Cathedral, yet it conveys a fine impression of the original crispness of its carving.

41

LIFE AND DEATH

PICTS AT HOME AND AT WAR

WHATEVER purpose the symbol stones fulfilled, it had little to do with the everyday lives of ordinary Picts. If they were memorials, the people thus commemorated were the wealthy and powerful minority; if they recorded marriage alliances, the partners came from aristocratic stock; if they marked boundaries, the lands were tribal. Even though the surviving stones can only be a proportion of those that once existed, there must have been many thousands more people than stones. This selective element comes through also in what is depicted on the stones: while the realistic animals reflect those familiar to all Picts, the realistic objects reflect the possessions of the favoured few, with the exception of the comb. Bone and antler combs are frequently found in excavations and ought to have been within the bartering power of many people, whereas bronze mirrors would have been expensive luxury items. Even the blacksmith's tools of hammer, anvil and tongs mark a craftsman whose standing in society is likely to have been high.

One of the most important possessions of an ordinary Pictish family must have been the axe, although it appears on the stones only in exceptional circumstances (e.g. the Rhynie man, p 6). Many of the most frequent Pictish placenames relate to forest and woodland—for example, names with the element *cardden*, meaning copse, as in Kincardine. Such placenames imply a heavily wooded landscape in which trees would have to be cut down to create new fields, and the wood used to build houses, carts, boats, furniture and endless small items (bowls, spoons, handles for tools). All this activity required the axe, probably the blacksmith's most sought-after product.

Unfortunately for the archaeologist trying to reconstruct a picture of everyday life among the Picts, wood rarely survives. Finding the right waterlogged conditions in which wood (and other organic materials such as leather) will survive is not easy and indeed is usually pure chance, but, until a Pictish settlement with such conditions is found, we can get some idea of what is missing by looking at contemporary sites farther afield. The ditch surrounding the early monastery on Iona yielded pieces of lathe-turned wooden bowls, and wet conditions on a crannog, a house on an artificial island, in Loch Glashan (Argyll) had preserved not only timbers of the house but also wooden equipment such as a paddle, bucket, trough, scoop, spoon and bowls. Not surprisingly

The back of the cross-slab from Aldbar (now in Brechin Cathedral) shows, at the top, a pair of robed figures sitting on the bench, its high back ornamented with carved terminals. Alongside the figures of David wrestling with a lion are carved two more wooden objects, a staff and a harp. This type of triangular harp is thought by some scholars to have been a Pictish invention.

Opposite
The rocky hill of Dundurn (Perth and Kinross) was ideally placed for a frontier fort to guard the route along Strathearn between Pictland and Dalriada.

43

perhaps, urban Dublin of the 10th and 11th centuries possessed a more sophisticated range of wooden products, many decorated, which includes writing tablets, boxes, toys and even ornamental parts of chairs and benches, but there is no reason to suppose that such items were not widespread in the British Isles even in earlier centuries. Several cross-slabs show decorative knobs, sometimes animal heads, on the backs of chairs or benches (e.g. **St Vigeans** no 11, see p 37; Aldbar, Brechin Cathedral). Furniture such as this is also depicted in illustrated manuscripts, raising the question of whether the sculptor was basing the design on something familiar from life or on something copied and exotic. The Dublin evidence suggests that elaborate chairs and benches may well have been part of the furniture of wealthy households.

If so, they would be seen in the large timber halls that we assume Pictish chiefs lived in, at least in the area between the Forth and the Moray Firth. We can only assume this, because no such Pictish hall has been excavated and identified, but the post-holes and wall bedding-trenches of such buildings are known from aerial photographs; excavations have shown timber halls to have been built by the Britons and Angles (e.g. **Doon Hill**, Dunbar, East Lothian), and the Picts are likely to have lived in similar style.

Their ancestors were certainly capable of building large circular wooden houses, and the change in tradition from round to rectangular seems to have taken place sometime in the middle of the first millennium AD. Part of a large rectangular building was uncovered within the Pictish fort at Green Castle, Portknockie, on the coast of Moray. Oddly enough, it is in the ramparts of such forts that we glimpse the carpentry skills of the Picts. One of the techniques used by the Picts in fort-building was to create a timber framework to strengthen a rampart of earth and stone; this was not a new idea, for it had been known for the previous thousand years in Scotland, but it was particularly suitable for the creation of impressive defences. Only the base of the burnt timbering survived at Portknockie, but it was enough to show that there had been a box-like framework of squared timber, with upright posts mortised into horizontal beams. At Burghead the beams in the rampart had been fastened together with long iron spikes.

Promontories were favourite locations for forts, underlining the importance to the Picts of access to the sea. Craggy inland hills were also fortified, sometimes re-using the sites of old iron-age forts such as Craig Phadrig near Inverness or Clatchard Craig near Newburgh in Fife (destroyed this century by quarrying), and sometimes building anew, as at Dundurn (Perth and Kinross), where a hilltop citadel dominates a series of fortified lower terraces.

The existence of forts and the records in monastic annals of battles and sieges testify to the warlike aspects of Pictish society, but very few weapons have survived. The only battle-scene on a symbol stone has been discussed already (**Aberlemno** churchyard, see pp 24-7), and it is a useful source of information about warriors and weapons. Shields are circular with protruding bosses that serve a dual purpose, both to protect the hand-grip behind and to convert the shield into an offensive weapon by being thrust into the face of the enemy. Spears have long shafts and can be thrown as javelins or held in the hand as thrusting weapons. Swords have pommels and hilt-guards, and their blades are relatively short and broad. There is an ornate silver sword-pommel in the St Ninian's Isle treasure (Shetland), along with two chapes or protective mountings for the tips of scabbards; the chapes are broad and rounded, and this suggests that the tips of the swords within their scabbards were similarly shaped. The treasure was buried around AD 800, and the sword fittings were thus contemporary with the carving of the **Aberlemno** slab. The use of such chapes is confirmed by the early 9th-century slab, **Meigle** no 3, on which a horse-borne warrior wears a sword beneath his outer garment, the tip of the scabbard protected by a broad chape.

Two exquisite scabbard-chapes were included in the 8th-century Pictish treasure found on St Ninian's Isle in Shetland (now in the Royal Museum of Scotland, Edinburgh). Made of gilded silver with blue glass eyes, they were designed to strengthen the tips of leather scabbards for swords. The chape on the left is inscribed with the Latin formula, INNOMINEDS, 'In the name of God the highest', and another inscription on the other side records that this splendid object was made for Resad, son of Spusscio, presumably two Pictish Shetlanders.

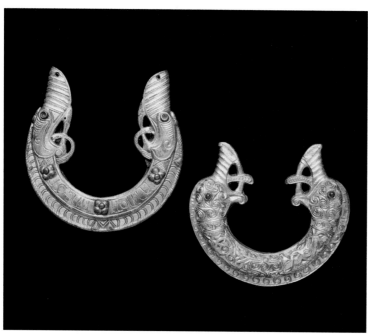

Looking at other stones, it is clear that, as well as circular shields, the Picts also used square or rectangular shields (e.g. **Eassie,** p 2; **Brough of Birsay,** p 54), and that spears were weapons for hunting as well as for battle (e.g. Hilton of Cadboll, p 9). Another hunting weapon was the crossbow (e.g. **St Vigeans** no 1; Shandwick), the strength of which was specially suited to hunting wild boar.

Boar and deer were animals hunted and presumably relished at table, as were salmon and perhaps geese. Domestic animals depicted on the stones include horses, bulls, cows, steers, sheep and hunting dogs. But for detailed information about Pictish diet and husbandry, we must turn to excavated Pictish homes. Like their forebears, the Picts were essentially farmers, relying primarily upon breeding cattle, sheep and pigs but growing cereal crops as well: our evidence comes from Orkney, where barley and oats were grown, but the arable element may have been stronger in southern Pictland. Domestic animals were important not just as sources of food, but for their hides (clothing, bedding, covering for skin-boats, vellum for manuscripts) and for their bones (combs, pins, knife-handles).

In the north of Pictland, particularly in the Northern Isles, the traditional building material was stone rather than wood, and houses were therefore more durable than farther south. Most of our information about Pictish houses comes from Orkney, from state-funded excavations undertaken in the 1970s and 1980s, and there are the reconstructed remains of a Pictish house at **Gurness**. One particularly important fact emerges from Pictish domestic life in the far north: symbols could be used informally on everyday objects and building slabs, not just on formal monuments and ceremonial silver finery. Playing-pieces for a board game could be decorated with symbols: one from **Jarlshof** (Shetland) bears a double-disc and Z-rod, and one from Burrian on North Ronaldsay (Orkney) bears a crescent and V-rod and a disc with indented rectangle symbol (both are in the Royal Museum of Scotland, Edinburgh). A stone from **Gurness**, apparently built into a wall, is incised lightly with three symbols (two rectangles and a disc with indented rectangle), while a paving slab from Pool on Sanday (Orkney) bears a double disc with an unfinished Z-rod. This slab lay face down as part of a large paved area that was built in the mid 6th century, and the significance of this early date is discussed on p 20.

This Pictish horseman looks a little cramped on the cross-slab, **Meigle** no. 3, but there are interesting details about his equipment: his sword-scabbard, half-hidden beneath his outer garment, has a rounded chape strengthening the tip, he sits on a striped saddle-cloth, his feet are shod in leather bootees with high tongues front and back, and he carries a spear at rest in his right hand.

Symbol stone from **Gurness**.

The archer on **St Vigeans** no. 1: his weapon is clearly a crossbow rather than a longbow, because his left hand is holding the broad wooden piece on which the arrow lies rather than the bow itself.

On the east coast of mainland Orkney, overlooking the sound between Mainland and the island of Rousay, lies the broch village of **Gurness**. The site had a long history of some 900 years, and most of the visible buildings belong to pre-Pictish times (described in another volume in this series, *Scotland BC*). The great broch, or stone tower, and its surrounding houses appear to have been deserted by about AD 400, and this once-thriving village fell into ruin. New inhabitants were attracted to the site around AD 600, perhaps because the ruins offered an easy source of building and even the chance, here and there, of making use of old walls still standing. These people were Picts, and they built a distinctive style of house quite different from the old sprawling village of their iron-age ancestors.

When **Gurness** was excavated in the 1930s, there were traces of Pictish buildings to the north and south of the broch, but inevitably these had to be removed in order to excavate the earlier levels beneath. None had survived much beyond the bottom courses of its walls, but one, to the south of the broch, was virtually intact in floor-plan, and this was carefully lifted, stone by stone, and re-built to the west of the excavated area (now in front of the site museum).

This house became known as the Shamrock, because its internal design of small rooms surrounding a central living area resembled the shape of a shamrock or clover leaf. It had been built with its foundations sunk into the rubble below and its walls of stone and turf combined: stone on the inside and at the doorway, backed on the outside by a thick blanket of turf blocks. No trace of the turf survived, of course, but the stonework was not substantial enough on its own for walls, and this technique of stone and turf combined is known from later times—it would have made a very snug and windproof house. From the outside, the house would have appeared circular or oval, as in the reconstruction drawing here. Turf would probably have been used for the roof-covering as well, as divots laid on a timber framework—in the drawing the roof is newly turfed and the individual divots are visible, but in time they would grow together and their edges become blurred. The low roof-pitch shown in the drawing is also based on old records of turf roofs in the Northern Isles.

There would have been a wooden door, probably set some way into the passage rather than at the very entrance; a pivot-stone on which such a door could swing was found, though not in position.

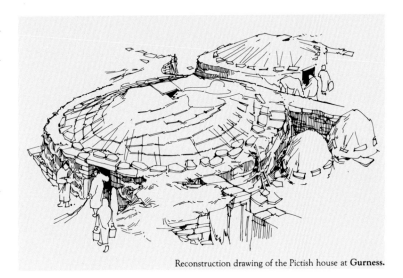

Reconstruction drawing of the Pictish house at **Gurness**.

Inside the house at **Gurness**.

Inside, the central focus of the house was the hearth, carefully built in typical Pictish fashion with a stone kerb and a paved base. Hearths were often furnished with a post-hole on either side to

Opposite
The reconstructed Pictish house at **Gurness**, Orkney, with the old broch in the background.

47

Gurness: the bronze-working area at the back of the Pictish house.

Gurness: an iron knife set in a bone handle; the ogam strokes incised on the handle are not translatable but they may identify the owners of the knife or they may have a talismanic meaning (Royal Museum of Scotland, Edinburgh).

This bone comb from Buckquoy, Orkney, is typical of the Pictish combs carved on symbol stones.

This was not so well preserved and had clearly been re-built several times, but its importance to the archaeologist lies in the fact that it held evidence of bronze-working. There were a number of clay moulds and a crucible: the moulds were for making the pins of penannular brooches and dress pins of a type that was fashionable in the 7th and 8th centuries. A similar date can be given to another important find, an iron knife with a bone handle on which an ogam inscription has been carved. The symbol stone already mentioned in the site museum is not closely datable but it could belong within the same two centuries or earlier, and it underlines the Pictish character of this phase of settlement at **Gurness**. A fragment of a more formal symbol stone was found on the beach not far from **Gurness**; it bears part of a mirror symbol.

Traces of two successive houses built in the same style as the cellular house at **Gurness** were excavated on the Point of Buckquoy in Birsay, Orkney. There they were succeeded by a larger and more sophisticated house in which a main living-hall was flanked by a circular storage room at one end and an extra rectangular room at the other. It shares the same basic design features with the cellular houses: the piers of masonry separating the rooms and helping to support the roof, and the well-built central hearth. Buckquoy was a farmstead flourishing in the 7th and 8th centuries AD.

Pictish houses in the Northern Isles were not all built to the distinctive plans seen at **Gurness** and Buckquoy. Some formed irregular housing 'blocks', with oval and sub-rectangular rooms, as at Howe, near Stromness in Orkney, where they were built into the ruins of earlier broch-period dwellings, and at Pool on Sanday (both excavations funded by Historic Buildings and Monuments). A place where Pictish houses ought to have survived is **Jarlshof** in Shetland: the long history of habitation here spans some 4000 years, from the 17th century AD back into prehistory, but there is little to show for the Pictish phase,

take the supports for a spit across the fire. This would have been the principal cooking and working area of the house, and the four little cells surrounding it would probably have been used for sleeping and storage. The pillars of stonework separating these cells had an even more important purpose in supporting the roof. When it was excavated, charcoal and peat ash were found in and around the hearth, the remains of the twigs and peat used for fuel.

The back of the house had been built against an old wall surviving from earlier times, and a doorway through it gave access to another building.

A Pictish house at Buckquoy, Orkney, during excavation: an entrance porch in the foreground leads into a small rectangular room; beyond lies the living-hall with its central hearth and at the far end of the house is a circular storage chamber.

Jarlshof, Shetland: a Pictish building on the western edge of the site consists of a circular room and storage cell, built with the lower courses of the walls below ground-level.

perhaps because the main focus of the settlement at that time lay to the south of the old broch where marine erosion has destroyed all trace. The only surviving buildings of this period appear to be workshops and storehouses rather than dwellings, but it is likely that people continued to live for as long as possible in the magnificent wheel-houses built by their ancestors. There are also traces of occupation at this period at **Clickhimin** (Shetland).

Evidence of Christianity rarely turns up in domestic contexts, but among the Pictish finds from **Jarlshof** is a broken piece of slate on which

A Pictish artist at **Jarlshof** drew an elaborate Christian cross on a piece of slate.

Painted pebbles from **Jarlshof.**

Painted pebble from Keiss, Caithness.

a fanciful cross sprouting spirals has been incised. Some Pictish artist made good use of the local slate for drawing: animals, boats, interlace patterns and even portraits like the fine young man on p 5 whose aristocratic profile echoes the chieftain on the **Brough of Birsay** symbol stone (see p 54). The boats are often assumed to be those of the Vikings, an increasingly familiar sight by the end of the 8th century in the Northern Isles, but they could equally well be Pictish vessels. Undoubtedly Pictish is a stone disc, perhaps a gaming counter, decorated with the double-disc and Z-rod symbol—for some reason, when this symbol is used on small objects rather than on stone monuments the Z-rod crosses the double-disc at right angles instead of a 45° angle.

Painted quartzite pebbles like the three found at **Jarlshof** are a common denominator among the possessions of ordinary Pictish households. They were probably charm-stones used to ward off evil and 'treat' sickness, and they have turned up on settlements in the Northern Isles and the northern mainland of Scotland from the first few centuries AD on into Pictish times. Not one of the twenty pebbles found to date has been painted with a recognisable symbol, a fact that suggests that this was not a usage for which symbols were considered appropriate.

The painted pebble from Keiss, a broch-site in Caithness, bears a saltire with dots between the arms, and this motif also decorates the hinge-end

Jarlshof: drawings of boats with high prows and sterns, masts and rigging. The upper boat is under sail, while the lower is coming into shore, its sail furled, oars up out of the water and steering rudder at work.

of an unusual brooch from another broch-site on that north-east coast, **Carn Liath** in Sutherland. This silver brooch is a native version of a popular type of Roman brooch, and it was probably made in the 4th or 5th century. Amongst the decoration is a double-disc symbol, possibly one of the earliest known. The brooch was found during excavations of the buildings clustered outside the broch, and it implies that people were living here into Pictish times.

One of the regrets of the archaeologist must be that the Picts did not believe in placing personal belongings in graves — had they done so, a few more Pictish weapons might have survived. The bulk of the population appears not to have been given any sort of formal burial for which evidence might remain. Only in Fife were whole communities of Christian Picts buried in cemeteries; elsewhere the identifiable burials are few and can only represent a small and restricted segment of society. Such burials are identifiable as Pictish either by scientific dating of the bones or by association of the grave with a symbol stone. People were buried as inhumations (unburnt), stretched full length in long grave-pits that were

sometimes lined and covered with stone slabs (long cists). The grave was marked on the surface by a rectangular or circular cairn of stones, often capped by a scattering of white quartz pebbles, and, at Dairy Park, Dunrobin (Sutherland), a symbol stone was placed upright on top. The finished monument would have been a fitting memorial for a member of a leading Pictish family.

Carn Liath: houses were built between the broch-tower and its encircling defensive rampart, and people continued to live here long after the need for the broch had passed.

Silver brooch from **Carn Liath,** Sutherland: a double disc symbol is visible on the decorative plate (replica, Royal Museum of Scotland, Edinburgh).

At the north-west tip of the mainland of Orkney lies the beautiful Bay of Birsay, its southern shore rising towards the great cliffs of Marwick Head and its northern side the promontory, Point of Buckquoy, that leads out to the tidal island known as the **Brough of Birsay**. The island presents a bleak face of 45-m high cliffs to the fury of Atlantic storms, but its landward image is a serene grassy slope. Most of the buildings visible today belong to Norse and early medieval times, but there was a thriving Pictish community living there long before the first Viking longship drew into the bay.

The most obvious clue to a Pictish presence is the symbol stone, a cast of which now stands within the graveyard (the original fragments are in the Royal Museum of Scotland, Edinburgh). Some of the decoration on the cast is conjectural, but there is no doubt that the stone bore the four symbols shown: the disc and rectangle (though the original rectangle could have been indented), the crescent and V-rod, the 'elephant' and the eagle, in that order from the top. Beneath the symbols is a splendid procession of three warriors in long robes.

Two myths have grown up around this stone since its discovery. One is that it marked the communal grave of three people corresponding to the three carved figures. A group of three graves side by side was excavated in the graveyard but it is clear that the stone did not originally stand at their head (as the cast does today). The other myth is that the surviving carved face of the stone was originally the back of a cross-slab and that the cross-face had

The surviving fragments of the symbol stone have been pieced together, with the missing parts of the symbols outlined on the modern background.

The Bay of Birsay and the **Brough of Birsay.**

Aerial view of the **Brough of Birsay**

somehow sheared off. Both myths are examples of 'the past as wished for': the triple grave as a neat explanation of the three carved warriors, and the missing cross-face as a rationalisation of an otherwise unique symbol stone. Most of the surviving fragments of the symbol stone were found together in their correct relative positions as if the major part of the stone had fallen complete and shattered as it fell, partly against the wall of the graveyard. It is difficult to envisage that the other side of the slab had sheared off previously, taking with it the carved cross — particularly as Orkney flagstone readily produces large thin slabs. More probably, this was not a cross-slab but a late symbol stone, a hybrid between the incised symbol stone and the relief cross-slab. Whether it was set up to mark a grave or for some other reason will never be known.

It was argued in the past that an early Christian monastic settlement existed on the Brough, but there is no conclusive evidence and opinion among scholars today tends to place more emphasis on the secular aspects of the community that undoubtedly lived there in the 7th and 8th centuries. The surviving church and graveyard belong to the 12th century, and evidence of earlier graves and walls may represent an 11th-century or earlier Norse foundation, but, apart perhaps from the symbol stone, there is nothing to prove a Pictish ecclesiastical presence. Nevertheless, an early church serving a princely household is an appropriate concept that could still be proved correct.

But who are the three warriors on the symbol stone? Dressed not for battle but in long formal

53

The three warriors — could this be an Orcadian chief with two of his retinue?

robes, they carry their weapons at rest almost like badges of office rather than tools of their trade. The sculptor has shown clear differences in status between them: the leader has an elaborately curled hairstyle, a highly decorated shield and a fringe or striped braid at the hem of his robe. His two followers wear plain robes, but the last man is beardless. The whole scene has been carved partly in low relief, and by dropping the edge of the pecked area beneath the butt of the leader's spear the carver has underlined his prominence once again. He has also added some technical details: the midrib on the leader's spearhead (in real life this would be made of iron with a socket into which the wooden shaft fitted), the central square boss on each shield and the four rivets by which the hand-grip was attached to the back of the shield. The edges of the shields appear to be bound, perhaps implying a wooden base with a leather or metal covering held together by a binding. The elaborate sword fittings of silver in the St Ninian's Isle hoard prove that costly weapons existed, and fragments of decorated silver sheeting in the Norrie's Law hoard (Fife) may have adorned a circular shield. All three warriors have swords hanging from their belts.

Clearly this hierarchy of three had some significance for the Pictish community at Birsay. Some scholars would see them as simply a repetition of conventional iconography, three figures from some biblical or saintly tale — but no other symbol stone compares with this one. Even if there had originally been a cross-face on the other side, this combination of symbols and figural panel is unique. It suggests that, for the carver, and for the audience, the three warriors had the status of a symbol. The attention to detail in the carving and the ceremonial air of the scene imply a real-life local significance as a depiction of an element of Pictish society. We are looking at a chieftain and two of his retinue, who may have been contemporary with the carving or may have been familiar figures from the past or simply symbols of kingship.

We know from historical records that Orkney had a ruler of more than local importance. When St Columba visited the court of the Pictish king, Bridei son of Maelchon, in AD 565, one of those present was the Orcadian king. Adomnan uses the term *regulus* rather than the more usual *subregulus* to describe this ruler, perhaps implying that his status was greater than that of a minor provincial king. We are also told that Bridei held hostages of this king, indicating that Orcadian power had to be held in check. It seems possible that the Orcadian royal family was one of the lineages from which potential future high kings of the whole of Pictland might be drawn.

The Brough of Birsay may well have been a residence of this Orcadian ruling family. As a tidal island its natural defences were excellent. The Birsay area is one of the most fertile parts of mainland Orkney, and the fact that it became a centre of secular and ecclesiastical power in Norse times may reflect an equivalent political importance in earlier times. Certainly there is archaeological evidence for a wealthy Pictish community on the Brough, in the form of debris from the production of fine jewellery.

During excavations in the 1930s, a small well was discovered within the area enclosed by the east annexe of the later churchyard. It is only 750 mm deep and an average 300 mm across, but it is carefully built of flat beach pebbles laid in horizontal courses, and it is the only Pictish structure visible on the Brough today. The old ground surface beside the well was covered with ashes, broken clay moulds, crucibles and fragments of coloured glass, clear evidence of metalworking activities in which the well may have played a part by supplying water for cooling and cleaning. Traces of buildings were uncovered both then and in later excavations in the 1970s and 1980s, to the north and east of the well, but not enough survived to give a reliable impression of the appearance of the Pictish settlement.

This small slab-lined well served a bronzesmith's workshop.

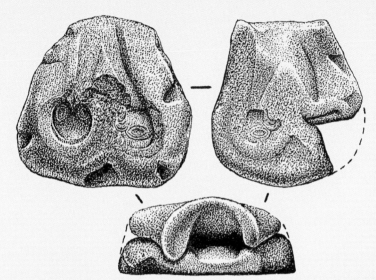

In contrast, the metalworkers have left a vivid picture of the jewellery commissioned by affluent patrons. Hundreds of broken pieces of moulds and complete moulds show that penannular brooches were the favourite items, cast in bronze and sometimes decorated with enamel or glass. There are very close stylistic links between the products of this workshop and the silver brooches in the St Ninian's Isle hoard. Few of the brooches made in the Birsay moulds have survived, for they would have become heirlooms to be passed on — or, if broken, the metal would have been melted down and used again. As well as brooches, other small items such as dress pins and finger rings were made, all in simple two-piece moulds. The bronze was melted in tiny clay crucibles of which at least sixty have survived, intact or broken, and fragments of thin bronze sheet show that objects of beaten bronze were produced as well as those cast in moulds. Bowls and other vessels made of beaten bronze or silver were popular in wealthy households.

At no time in its history, Pictish or Norse, can the community living on the Brough have been self-sufficient in terms of food. Supplies of grain and meat would have been imported from mainland farms such as Buckquoy, which could even have belonged to the princely household on the Brough. If in the future more excavation takes place there, the feasting hall of Pictish times may yet be found, but in the meantime the symbol stone and the evidence of metalworking are enough to show that the Brough of Birsay was the home of one of the leading families of 8th-century Pictland.

Above
A silver penannular brooch from the St Ninian's Isle hoard.

Above top
A two-piece mould for a penannular brooch from the **Brough of Birsay**; the two halves fit together, leaving a gap or 'gate' at the top onto which the molten bronze could be poured (the edges would be sealed with clay).

Left
A lead disc, 50 mm across, decorated with a spiral pattern, from the **Brough of Birsay.**

Opposite
Meigle no. 2, back: even the
blurring effect of weathering
cannot hide the astounding
visual impact that this stone,
freshly cut, must have
possessed. The deep relief and
orderly arangement of the
figures is the work of a master
sculptor.

Meigle no. 2: the form of the
cross-head is unique, based
perhaps on a metal jewelled
cross.

A CULTURE OBLITERATED

WHAT HAPPENED TO THE PICTS?

THE kingdom of the Picts came to a gradual end during the first half of the 9th century AD. Although most of Pictland became Scotland at the hands of an old adversary, Dalriada, the decisive factor was a new and mutual enemy, the Vikings. Viking raids along the northern and western coasts began in the last decades of the 8th century — the first recorded raid was on Iona in 795 — and the Scandinavian settlement of the islands of northern Pictland and northern Dalriada was underway soon afterwards. Pictland shrank as Shetland and Orkney were lost, and tiny Dalriada was all too conscious of its vulnerable position on the western seaways along which Viking ships sailed to loot the rich monasteries of Ireland.

Not for the first time, Dalriada looked eastwards.

Succession to the Pictish throne had already fallen legitimately in the late 8th century to kings of Scottish blood, and this trend continued during the early part of the 9th. It seems likely that small numbers of Scots came eastwards to settle in Pictland, introducing new ideas such as the sculptural influence visible on the **Fowlis Wester** cross-slab but not altering the political character of their adopted land. This changed around AD 843, when Kenneth mac Alpin established Scottish royal, political and cultural supremacy — historical sources are ambiguous on the subject of precisely when and how this was achieved, to what extent warfare was involved, but its effect was permanent. There is documentary and place-name evidence to suggest that some aspects of Pictish administration and land tenure continued to exist under Scottish rule, and commonsense demands that a mixture of language and culture persisted for a generation or two. Sculpture provides the only visual record of the effect of the

Meigle no. 2, back: the central figure is Daniel surrounded by lions.

Right
Meigle no. 1: the cross with its interlace filling is surrounded by animals.

Opposite
Meigle no. 1, back: an oddly uncoordinated panel in which symbols and exotic motifs seem carelessly scattered in and around a hunting scene.

political takeover and of the arrival of significant numbers of Scots seeking a new life away from the immediate threat of the Norsemen.

Like the collection at **St Vigeans**, the sculptures now housed in the old school at **Meigle** (Perth and Kinross) imply that there was once a major church or even monastery nearby. There is an historical reference to the work of Thana, son of Dudabrach, at Meigle around AD 840, and it is possible that Thana was a scribe based in a monastery which, to judge by the surviving stones, could well have been founded in the 8th century. The stones were found close to or in some cases built into the old church that was destroyed by fire in 1869, and several more stones were recorded in the last century than survive today — including a unique carving of a chariot on a slab that was probably designed to be part of a decorative frieze on a building.

The museum is dominated by three great cross-slabs, one of which (no 2) has the odd feature of projecting tenons on its sides and top, as if designed to slot into a screen or wall or perhaps a frame. Some of the stones bear symbols, but most of the pieces belong to the 9th or 10th centuries and are tombstones, including an exceptionally fine horizontal or recumbent graveslab (no 26), with a socket at one end to hold an upright cross or slab. There are exotic elements to rival those on the **St Andrews** sarcophagus: the Persian god and camel portrayed on cross-slab no 1 must have been copied from some imported treasure. The horsemen on several stones are particularly interesting for the detailed representation of their

equipment (see p 45 for no 3); the local sandstone was a perfect medium for fine sculpture.

The sculptural traditions at monastic centres such as **Meigle** and **St Andrews** survived the political upheavals of the 9th century by dropping the now redundant symbols and adopting new fashions. Elsewhere the political threat gave rise to huge nationalistic symbols for a time, usually on the wayside cross-slabs commissioned by secular patrons, and their message is clear. Good examples are the **Aberlemno** roadside cross-slab (see p 26) and the **Maiden Stone**. These dominating symbols are in sharp contrast to the small and apologetic symbols tucked inconspicuously into the overall design on slabs such as **Dunfallandy** (see p 29).

The **Maiden Stone** (Gordon) is a typical 9th-century cross-slab. The cross itself occupies just the central portion of a tall and narrow slab, with

a figural scene above (probably Jonah escorted by a pair of whales) and a large panel of intricate patterning below. Both narrow sides are decorated, one with interlace and the other with triangular knotwork, and the back is divided into panels dominated by huge symbols. The simplicity of design on the back is in stark contrast to the rest of the stone and all the more powerful as a result.

Later cross-slabs show no Pictish symbols, although they were still the work of Pictish craftsmen under new masters or at least in a new political climate. The mixture of Pictish and

Meigle no. 22: part of an architectural frieze with a Pictish version of the Celtic god, Cernunnos, in classic cross-legged pose, but here his legs have become elongated and end in fish-tails and his horns have become serpentine coils.

Opposite
Meigle no. 4: the fragments that survive of this cross-slab are still crisply carved, and there is a pleasing symmetry about the two animals on either side of the top of the cross, their necks arching back to bite the two creatures framing the slab.

61

Fowlis Wester (Perth and Kinross): the side-arms of the cross protrude beyond the edge of the slab in Irish fashion. Fully 3 m tall, the detailed carving is badly weathered (the iron chain is probably the remains of a jougs or iron collar by which miscreants were held in medieval times for all to see). The back is full of lively scenes, including a pair of huntsmen riding abreast, one with a hawk on his arm. The double disc and Z-rod at the top and the crescent and V-rod lower left are almost incidental.

Right

The **Maiden Stone,** Chapel of Garioch (Gordon), a tall cross-slab of pink granite traditionally linked with a daughter of the laird of Balquhain. The story tells how she made a wager with a stranger that she could bake a good supply of bread before he could build a road to the top of Bennachie: the stranger turned out to be the Devil in disguise, finished the road before the bread was ready and returned to claim her as his reward, but she fled before him and was transformed into stone as he caught her. The carving is sadly weathered, especially on the cross-face, but it is still possible to appreciate its former beauty.

Far right

Maiden Stone, back: beneath a weathered panel of animals, massive symbols demand attention (a notched rectangle and Z-rod, an 'elephant' and a mirror and comb).

Scottish traditions is clearly seen on the splendid great monument at Forres in Moray, **Sueno's Stone**: though very tall, this is still a cross-slab rather than a free-standing cross and its decoration includes not only the vine-scroll dear to Pictish tradition but also the panels filled with rows of figures that are typical of 10th-century Irish crosses. This is a graphic memorial of a great battle. The fort at **Burghead**, only 12 km away on the Moray coast, was violently destroyed in the 9th or 10th century, perhaps as a result of that same battle. But whether this was Pict against Scot or both against the Norseman, neither archaeology nor history can tell.

Sueno's Stone (Moray): this exceptionally tall and intricately carved cross-slab has been described as 'a fitting close to the great sculptural school of the Moray Firth area'. This remarkable monument will be treated fully in the next volume in this series.

FURTHER READING

J Close-Brooks, *The Highlands*, Edinburgh, 1986.

J Close-Brooks and R B K Stevenson, *Dark Age Sculpture*, Edinburgh, 1982.

J G P Friell and W G Watson, *Pictish Studies: settlement, burial and art in Dark Age Northern Britain*, Oxford, 1984.

I Henderson, *The Picts*, London, 1967.

A Jackson, *The Symbol Stones of Scotland*, Kirkwall, 1984.

E Meldrum (ed), *The Dark Ages in the Highlands*, Inverness, 1971.

I Ralston and J Inglis, *Foul Hordes: the Picts in the North-East and their background*, Aberdeen, 1984.

A Ritchie, *The Kingdom of the Picts*, Edinburgh, 1977.

A Ritchie, *Orkney and Shetland*, Edinburgh, 1985.

A Ritchie, *Scotland BC*, Edinburgh, 1988.

G Ritchie and A Ritchie, *Scotland: archaeology and early history*, London, 1981.

I A G Shepherd, *Grampian*, Edinburgh, 1986.

A Small (ed), *The Picts: a new look at old problems*, Dundee, 1987.

A Small and L M Thoms, *The Picts in Tayside*, Dundee, 1985.

F T Wainwright (ed), *The Problem of the Picts*, Edinburgh, 1955 (reprinted Perth, 1980).

A P Smyth, *Warlords and Holy Men*, London, 1984.

B Walker and G Ritchie, *Fife and Tayside*, Edinburgh, 1987.

ACKNOWLEDGEMENTS

We are indebted to the following institutions and individuals for permission to reproduce photographs: Royal Commission on Ancient Monuments, Scotland (pp 8, 11); Royal Museum of Scotland, Queen Street, Edinburgh, courtesy of the Trustees of the National Museums of Scotland (pp 19, 44, 52, 55); Ian A G Shepherd (p 12); Graham Ritchie (pp 49, 55). Drawings were kindly provided by David Pollock (p 47) and T Borthwick (pp 5, 10, 54, 55), and the text was kindly typed by Jane Gough.

INDEX OF PLACES MENTIONED IN THE TEXT

Printed in Scotland for HMSO by C.C.No. 61484, 9/90, Dd 0287711, C50.